T0365793

LUCIFER THE LION

The Lightbearer

Reverend Tracy L Crowe

Balboa Press books may be ordered through booksellers or by contacting:

Balboa Press
A Division of Hay House
1663 Liberty Drive
Bloomington, IN 47403
www.balboapress.com
1 (877) 407-4847

ISBN: 978-1-4525-9008-0 (sc)
ISBN: 978-1-4525-9007-3 (e)

Library of Congress Control Number: 2014900161

Printed in the United States of America.

Balboa Press rev. date: 5/30/2014

BALBOA
PRESS
A DIVISION OF HAY HOUSE

DEDICATION

This book is dedicated to Mark Pritchard, Member of Parliament for Great Britain. Mr. Pritchard your continued advocacy and dedication to animal welfare is an inspiration for many of us and I hope this book will give you even more inspiration and energy to continue your amazing endeavors.

Secondly, I dedicate this book to the many animals that have graced my life and made a difference in opening up my heart and giving me purpose throughout all of the trying times from childhood through my career. Thank all of you for being there for me and the unconditional love that you shared. I loved and greatly miss all of you. Darn you for not having longer lifespans.

Also, I want to share a very heartfelt thank you to Ms. Amanda Wamunyima, who is currently the reigning Ms. Florida America 2014. She is the former Miss Zambia USA 2010, and by the grace of God, soon to be Ms. America. Amanda thank you for your exuberant support and dedication to the quality of life for rescued animals.

SPECIAL THANK YOU

I would like to take this opportunity to thank J. Brown, J.D. and Joe Margio for their support and thought provoking, critical comments.

NOTE:

Many of you that will read this first book of mine are extremely literate. I ask you to forgive a soul that is not a literature buff, and that is spending all of her own savings to write this book to help rescued animals. I could not afford an editor this time around, but I promise you Virgos, Capricorns, Scorpios and Geminis that I will hire an Editor for any future books.

CONTENTS

PREFACE

Many of us get to points in life, where we feel like we have either accomplished a lot of great things but wonder if it is enough and what is the next step, or maybe we feel like we have not accomplished anything that we intended. Even better, some are just starting out and have no idea where to begin. I fell into the accomplished a lot. I had hit the top ceiling in my career, as far as I could. I was the President of a successful design firm for almost 15 years, with up to eighteen employees to take care of. I was the sole owner and I sold the business. The week that I sold it, I had the "terrible three" happen. Many of you have heard the expression that when bad things start to happen they happen in the threes. My three brought me to my knees begging "my creator" to please explain why and open the doors for me to understand what to do. I was a huge success in this world of material things. Essentially retired at a very young age and had the money now to take care of my aging mother. Yet I was alone and completely lost on what to do next.

I want to be clear and honest. I was neither a religious nor spiritual person when this happened. Not that I had never attended church, or attempted to read the Bible, it is just that I had let my career take over my life and it had become my only priority. In addition, almost nothing had resonated with me about religion, since my Uncle passed away, who was an amazing Preacher. Simply because he was humble, real and spoke from his heart. I had not discovered someone to "move me" that way again, so I guess I gave up.

Let's just say my path has become illuminated since that time, and this is the story of how the universe showed me that I had a purpose greater than any material job or being the head of any company making money could ever fulfill.

I am a first time writer. Ironically, this is not the first book I have written. The first book will tell in detail about the day I started to realize all of these synchronicities and where that path took me in the beginning. However, I realized that this book and its cause to help animals in captivity was much more important than sharing my personal story first, although I think both will have impacts on those that read it that need to hear it and would like a boost of hope and faith in their lives right now. We can make a difference as an individual, and each one of us does have a purpose for being here. I hope with all my heart that you find your purpose from the help of this book, or that you are already home.

INTRODUCTION

This book is broken into three parts. Part I tells you that there is a need to help animals in captivity that are held in completely inadequate facilities, and uses a specific example of rare endangered lions. I felt it was important for the reader to understand upfront the purpose for the writing of this book the possibility for all of us to make a difference.

Part II of this book is my own personal spiritual path that shares the facts about how amazingly I was lead to these lions through following everyday signs and synchronicities. It also shows how I learned to overcome fear and find my true purpose for being here. A second purpose contained in Part II is to assist any reader that finds themselves in the same place that I was when I began this amazing journey to find the hope necessary to follow their own path of destiny.

Lastly, Part III tells about the amazing progress that has happened as a result of following the signs and obtaining the courage to engage in activities and meet with people and try to make a difference. All the doors are opening wide, there is more of my personal spiritual path in Part III, and I think the reader will be amazed to hear how the universe will help you when you start doing what makes your heart sing.

PART I

THE ISSUE

THE ISSUE

The biggest issue that I discovered through all that happened was the acute need for a shift. First it had to happen in my own thinking, but then I yearn that it will happen for all of us. When I say a shift, yes I mean the cliché "paradigm shift", but there is no better way to say that "I had to stop employing typical assumptions that this world had programmed into my head."

I must first admit that I love animals. All types of animals. Of course, many of us tend to have a larger affinity at first toward the furry and fuzzy ones, as they say in Bugs Bunny, we want to "hug them and squeeze them and call them George." However, I am one of those characters that can relate when a snake feels scared or cold and also have a special affinity for the wellbeing of the less favored of the lot. Thank God for Walt Disney making mice special, or we may never have gotten over the mothers of the world just wanting to beat the hell out of them with brooms when they appeared in their kitchens; instead they became a favorite for many children.

I have raised several small animals throughout my life and I have always been attracted to going to zoos around the world. The thing is that when I was at a zoo, from a very young age, I felt like I would look into the animals soul through their eyes. I was never one that could stand other children coming up beside me and banging on the glass and making faces and teasing the animals. I do not know what made me different, and why I did not join in with the other children. There were many of the animals that I would find miserable when I looked in their eyes, but I was programmed to believe that is just the way it is supposed to be in our society with animals in small cages behind glass or bars, even though it seemed horribly wrong, and that nothing gave us any power as individuals to do anything about it.

As an adult, I continue to be attracted to animals and went to a zoo whenever an opportunity arose. I always left somber and as sad for the animals as when I "used" to allow myself to visit a petstore, before I became aware like everyone else how abused animals are in those petmills. Luckily, we went through that paradigm shift and let everyone clearly know through amazing marketing campaigns how awful those petstore facilities can be. Thank you to the people who took a stand and did something to make a change in that perception and save countless animals from the same fate of ending up in petstores. I know, we still have a long way to go on that front, but let us stay focused on the positive. We have made some strides as a society.

Back to the zoo issue - I have seen animals in amazing preserves, or what seemed to be adequate zoo habitats that seemed to be thriving. However, I have learnt so much that goes on behind the scenes now from organizations that care. Many of those happy looking animals will not even breed in captivity because it is so out of their normal environment, or may be slowly going insane inside because their habitat is not suitable for their geographic and instinctual behavior patterns.

So here is the paradigm – Whenever I see animals in public facilities that are simply inadequate facilities and I feel in my heart they are miserable, I had a specific response that always came to my mind. See if in your heart this resonates with you, as well. I thought "why doesn't this damn zoo or the government do something about this." Excuse my American (not "French", we cuss enough to start blaming ourselves, right?), but have you ever thought something similar?

Well you will read in Part II of this book, the journey and research I went through to change my angry assumptions (paradigm), and hopefully you will laugh with me about how my first reaction was to attack the zoo, the government and the people of the country I was in and demand "they" do something immediately.

Luckily, I stopped and "thought" before I did any damage running my sometimes over courageous and definitely over protective mouth. I came to realize the big picture. From all of my years of working as a hired expert to help governments improve their services to their constituents, I knew very well that my government is just an extension of me, of us. Any facility that a government operates is doing so under its constituent's supervision and direction. We are the "supervisors" that say we want more services, but we do not want to pay for them, do not tax us anymore. I am not pointing blame at us either. We as supervisors have been bitten many times over the centuries by wastes of money and we have lost trust, right? We work hard for our money and even religions state that you should only have to give a tithe (which translates to 10% by the way), so why the heck do we give so much more than ten percent in taxes and not get everything done. So there you have it, the issue. There is a substantial and sometimes well founded lack of trust, a problem with too many demanded services and not enough money and a desire to blame entities that are under "our" very control. Do not get depressed, here comes the solution.

THE SOLUTION

If we as humanitarians are ready to make a difference, here is how we get around the problem of government and take care of major issues that are near and dear to our hearts' ourselves. First, we see an inadequacy.

Second, we decide not to ignore it. It may be as simple as telling the right person, making a YouTube to share, praying or actually taking a stand and developing a campaign to correct an injustice or public safety issue. EVERY SINGLE HUMAN BEING ON EARTH HAS THE POWER TODAY TO MAKE A DIFFERENCE. As you will read, I chose to start a campaign. What we should not do and will do absolutely no good, is blame anything or send any negative thoughts. The energy and power of our thoughts have extremely powerful manifesting capacity, therein lays the power of prayer that has created miracles that have been witnessed around the world.

The other misconceived issue that often arises to cause delays or gridlock for doing a good cause is boundaries. We like to hide from making something our responsibility by saying it is that City's, or Country's or Race's issue not mine. "They" are terrible, why don't "they" do something about it. Let me make a couple points. The animals in zoos, circuses and entertainment are there for us. That is right – "us" – even if we do not visit them, they are held there in case we want to visit. The animals do not belong to the country or city or race. They are simply in a geographic location on earth and need someone around the world to care enough to build them something beautiful or release them and let mother nature do what she does best. The worldwide web is helping to drop these boundaries, but it will take us making up our minds for the true shift to occur; **compassion without boundaries**.

We have to address needs, not ignore them, and realize that it is actually our problem and not one of government (unless we make it their problem). Democratic governments should respond to the will of the people, or expect to be voted out of office, but we do not even have to go down that road; it is our problem, we are the public and we have the power to create projects and change situations without going through our government budgets. This is an extreme paradigm shift for us to be willing to take the responsibility for needs in our community, but we can do it if we want to.

Be honest with yourself about this one -- if we did not believe in government at all, we could create a list of the needed projects, prioritize them and decide collectively which we would fund and how much we would contribute. Right? However, here is the breakdown with that utopian model: some of us would not necessarily trust ourselves to do the contribution hoping that our richer neighbor will pay for it all right? That is why we created governments in the first place, with a demand for taxation, to ensure public projects get done and we are protected. When we can start trusting "ourselves" again, like communities that get together and build community buildings and facilities on the weekends, we will not need government. We can start collectively praying for that day to come, but I'm not sure it will arrive in my lifetime. In the meantime, we can support independently-funded projects outside a now overly bureaucratic government.

Next I am going to give you an example, of one such project that I came across, through what I would refer to now as a spiritual pilgrimage that I took through Europe during the summer of 2012.

ASIATIC LIONS IN LONDON

There is so much I could say about the glory of lions. The King of the Jungle has a roar that can be heard from FIVE miles away. I have literally stood in front of one when it roared, and my entire body vibrated and it took a while for me to get my breath back. They have been a representation of nobility for centuries in many cultures and revered creatures demonstrating great power on temples throughout antiquity.

However, in the seventeenth century, Monarchs of England kept lions in small confinements in the Tower of London for entertainment, and the public was allowed to come and feed them cats and dogs according to Wikipedia. They were transferred to the London Zoo in 1828, which is the location where my story starts.

I was fortunate enough from the sale of my business to have time off and to travel to Europe during the summer of 2012 which culminated with the 2012 Olympics in London. As a tourist during the Olympics, it was incredibly difficult to even locate the entrance to the London Zoo coming from the Tube (the subway). I did not see anything about the Zoo advertised at my hotel in downtown London to attract a visitor, and most British that I spoke to had not been to visit the zoo for 20 years and were unaware that there are rare Asiatic Lions with brand new cubs at the Zoo. There was no directional signage from the station to the zoo for pedestrians. After locating the boundary of the zoo, I was shocked by the way visitors were forced to enter the zoo. I made two failed attempts to enter at entrances that had ugly vertical turn styles that caused a sense of claustrophobia. Then the entrance to the zoo has no prominence or stature itself and is an outmoded design for modern parks today. It gave more of an impression of an entrance to someone's private zoo than to the Country's international zoo entrance.

I am familiar with many other international Zoo's, and I know that whether it is the country's capital city or just any other major cities Zoo, the Lions are often used as a prominent marketing feature for attracting visitors to the zoo. In this case, there was nothing prominent about the lion at the entrance. There is in Trafalgar Square in downtown London, but unfortunately the two public facilities are not tied together through any marketing.

Trafalgar Square (One of 4 giant lions)　　　　　*Another International Zoo Entrance*

Once I figured out the entrance, and I came across the Lion's environment in the London Zoo, I was shocked. These are images of the Lion's environment in the London zoo. The area is covered in trash and the water feature looks less than appealing because of the green scum that had accumulated (this was during the 2012 Olympics).

I know that animals have more instinct than humans about pollution and I am sure that it is stressful and harmful to be stuck in an enclosure where trash is left behind and not landscaped/groomed, besides polluted water. The picture on the next page of the father lion and two lionesses in a concrete enclosure, with no grass that is very old and the walls are falling apart. Even under the conditions, I witnessed the lion be a sweet father and let his cubs play with him and lick his face, before he rolled over for them and cleaned his face off. What a sweet guy.

This enclosure area is housing five of the rarest Asiatic lions in captivity and from what I could experience they could never have taken a run or truly stretched their legs. You can tell that the picture I took below was taken behind a glass wall. What this means is that visitors are allowed to approach the glass on both sides of this enclosure and, since there is no security present, let their children (and worse adults) bang on the glass all day long. Lions are supposed to sleep an enormous amount of hours each day in the wild, you can witness above how close everyone is to the actual Lion, which is unnecessary and unhealthy for the animals.

When the enclosure is this dark and unkempt and the landscaping is destroyed, it obviously creates a negative energy and visitors are not drawn to it. There were no plans being prepared or marketed to attract money that was desperately needed to expand the antiquated and undersized habitat even with the new cubs.

So that was the issue I was faced with and by comparison, I wanted to show you some images from another international zoo. Below is an exhibit that attracts numerous visitors all year round and the gift shop even has lines for the lion purchases only, with an entire gift shop dedicated predominantly to the lions close to their habitat. It is free to enter this zoo, it is all based upon donations and government funds.

Please note the landscaping and clean water, and happy active males living together in harmony. Please note these are not rare Asiatic lions, these are African lions that are becoming rare quickly due to loss of habitat too.

Although a safari or preserve would be preferable, there is at least room in this urban zoo for a good leg stretch below. Notice that they are attracting plenty of visitors in the background, which is well worth the investment.

So getting back to the issue in the London Zoo - The zoo estimated a need of 5 million Euros to redesign the habitat properly, please refer to Part III for details. There are 7 million people in London alone, forget about how many in England. If they all gave less than one pound in Euro it would solve the issue. If we are humanitarians, and want to recognize a world of unity (One) without country boundaries and we realize those boundaries do not exist in the world of these 5 lions, then it is less than a US penny for each of us around the world to make the necessary difference they need for this project.

The issue is awareness, and we have the worldwide web now, so now it is our problem to let people know these animals needs help. We also need to spread the word that we/humans are the biggest threat to the extinction of lions.

The round circle is a mirror

PART II

MY SPIRITUAL CONNECTION WITH GREAT BRITAIN'S LION

Now that you have been introduced to the issue about the lion in Part I, let me back up and tell you how I came about meeting this lion, his family, and what got me involved in doing something about it.

MY SPIRITUAL PATH

In light of all that happened, I feel compelled to share my story about the summer of 2012. Prior to April of 2012, all of my friends and family would have said I was probably not the spiritual type and pretty much "black and white", meaning that I needed to see things to believe them. But when I started telling these same friends what all was beginning to happen around me, they started repeating "I hope you are writing all of this down."

If someone else was telling ME the facts that I am about to share with you below, I may not have allowed myself to believe they were telling me the truth a year ago. However, I am writing this for a purpose greater than myself. I am doing it to save a family of lions and therefore I would like to share some curious synchronicities on my "path" for everyone to read. I usually consider myself a pretty private person and would not normally surrender to this exposure, but this is different.

> Please note that since I am writing about the "path" taken by a human being, I have to tell you the steps and spiritual signs as they occurred for me in a nearly chronological order, therefore, the reader will feel sometimes that nothing is connected and that I am jumping all over the place, but I assure you that all the connections and "lack of coincidences" are apparent in the end. I will try to bold some key words throughout to help.

THE PAINTINGS, THE BIBLE AND THE AFRICAN BOOK

It began in Grand Cayman. My cousins from Atlanta told me that I had to take time to visit Guy Harvey's art design studio on the island while I was visiting. I was slightly familiar already with Guy Harvey's talent and beautiful artworks. I knew he utilized his art work often to raise awareness for ocean conservation and to save the ocean's creatures. I went to the studio on the last day that I was visiting the island and I took a business associate with me. It was both amazing and ironic to discover that the one person I had invited with me had actually years before gone fishing with Guy Harvey off the shores in the country of Panama. Before I could even think about this amazing coincidence, my friend was re-introducing himself to Mr. Harvey while I slipped off to view the artwork throughout the studio by myself.

I had been looking for a painting for one wall of my house on the second story for nearly eight years. It's a large area and everything that I had found to date I felt was inordinately expensive due to the size of the wall and my own particular taste, so the wall had gone undecorated for all those years. In Guys Harvey's art studio I came across an entire wall of beautiful paintings, many small paintings that were amazing colors of turquoises and yellows. It was both the most beautiful artwork I had found to date and the most cost effective option by far. It was as if our creator had put them in my hands and whispered "these paintings are meant for you!" Plus my family back in Atlanta and close friend here with me in Grand Cayman have connections to Mr. Harvey, which hopefully means special signature, right?

When the shipment of paintings finally arrived, I had to start on my path to get them **hung on the wall** which was not a small task. It's a high wall and I knew I would have to hire help to get them hung that high up.

The next day, as I was walking through my own living room, where the paintings were laying on the floor, I noticed a copy of a National Geographic magazine laying in my magazine rack in my living room. The cover struck me right away. It was the "only" magazine in the rack, and I never remembered seeing it before that instance or receiving it in the mail. It had the King James Version of the bible on the front cover. I was drawn to it right away, since I had just started to awaken to all of these spiritual synchronicities and I had many questions. Like I said, I had been extremely black/white and science/math oriented toward the world not spiritual, so I was more likely to trust National Geographic than the Bible for "facts." I felt the immediate need to read the cover story about the Bible, which entailed a 4-page fold out detailing the numerous times the Bible had been translated and the many religions that had partaken in the translation and interjections into the Bible. I felt like again my Creator was giving me a quick lesson to know that the Bible was the original word, but that I would have to dig very deep into myself to determine what was left of the true word.

The more signs I was shown in the next couple of days made me draw conclusion that a "fear of God" had been written into the Bible, rather than the love and light that I personally feel with our Creator. I cannot explain how I just always knew intuitively that fear comes from evil thoughts and not from my Creator. It was the answer to a burning question I had always had since when I was very young. Second, it was made clear to me one of the questions I have always had, through my exposure to any religion or the Bible that clearly women appear to have been written out of the Bible. After that discovery, I was quickly drawn to several books and literature [even books on my own library shelves that I had never even given a moment's notice before and do not even know how I ended up with them] and, as if the universe was providing the answers to me, I found myself gravitating toward many sources that had already stated these same conclusions about fear not coming from "the original Word" and the clear omission of women's roles in the Bible. These book subjects, like sacred geometry, numerology and alchemy, were extremely complex for me to be able to suddenly understand them so quickly, and I had never had an interest in their subjects. It became so simple for me to comprehend that my Creator is pure love and we tend to be the ones that manifest so-called evil (such as lack, suffering, pain and oppression) with our thoughts. I was learning that we have the ability to change energy with our minds into negative matter. Likewise, we know that women are capable of equally thinking and expressing love and spiritual leadership, so the experience of "religions" had never made sense to me in these regards.

CLAIR-WRITING

This insert is going to seem disjointed and goes back in time a little, but it will make a lot of sense later. At this time something parallel had started happening for me. First of all, because I started to speak like an open book, I began to learn that many of my friends were already aware of these spiritual connections in their own lives and I was introduced or met many new individuals with many similar stories to my synchronicities or paranormal experiences. All these doors were opening for me, and I was told by many that they could tell I had strong psychic abilities. I always came back at them that I did not know what they were talking about, and then someone suggested a book that taught me how to do what is referred to as clair-writing… Clair-writing essentially boils down to asking the universe (in my case I choose to ask angels), questions in writing and then closing your eyes and getting a written response. It is freaking amazing. My hands could not stop writing and for the first time in my life I did not know the end of the sentence before I got around to writing it (my friends know my mind races and I do a lot of multi-tasking). With my "normal" writing, I am stuck in my own mind and almost always thinking two sentences ahead before I get around to writing them which makes me miss words and spell poorly until I proofread (I have had many employees that could attest to that). I cannot explain how different this clair-writing experience was. It felt clearly to me as though the responses were not from my own mind, but some deeper knowledge. With practice, I eventually began to have enough faith in my capability to do this writing that I "evolved" to leave my eyes open and even type the responses from the "angels or spirit guides"…

Well, based upon what I kept reading about in all these new books, one of the tasks in this new clair-writing skill that I wanted to tackle was to learn the names of my own guardian angels. I was told that everyone is born with at least two, and I wanted to know mine, so I received the names Jeremiah and **Lucy**, and I was absolutely thrilled and started practicing writing to them quite a bit before the paintings arrived. Then to be honest I got a little cocky with it and wanted to start helping friends discover the names of their guardian angels. So one of my guy friends allowed me to work with him and I came up with the names Vincent and **Mel**. He is Italian so that is no real surprise, but, again I cannot explain why, but I felt intuitively like his guardian angels were the energy of a male and **a female**, like mine. I asked the universe in front of my guy friend as we were driving to give us signs that it was Vincent and Mel. Suddenly, a large truck pulled out in front of us that said "Vinny's Towing" or something similar. We just looked at each other with our mouths open.

Still feeling cocky, I then decided to help a close girlfriend discover her guardian angels names. She is not a stranger to psychic abilities and was helping me decipher all of these new things happening in my life. She has a much deeper understanding of the spiritual connections than I even imagined, but she said she just never asked for the names of her guardian angels. She gave me permission, so one night, I began clair-writing at home alone and asked for the names of her guardian angels. I had gotten to a point already of being a strong believer in my Creator and the angels obviously (but that I will write more detail about another time), and I had learned to feel very safe and eliminate a lot of fear. This instance brought a lot of fear back quickly that night. As I began to write her guardian angels names, I wrote Ezekiel and stopped. The name of her second guardian angel I could only write down a "blank" space, I was too steeped in fear to put it in words. Feeling the onset of a complete panic attack, standing up, pacing, rubbing my head and putting my hands over my open mouth, mentally asking the universe "WHY, why are you telling me to write that, how can you say that? (I know I sound crazy talking to myself, but I'm really not, I'm talking to the universe of masters and spirit guides with 100% faith they are listening because of the reactions that occur). In my opinion, this close girlfriend is and always has been for nearly two decades as close as you can get on earth to "an angel" in my eyes. I do not think she would hurt a fly and I have never seen her lose her temper. However, I could not deny that the thought had just come to me strongly to write the word "Lucifer" as the name of her other guardian angel. I could not allow myself to write it and it is still blank in that journal entry to this day. I had never doubted the responses I had gotten before that moment, I had had complete faith in my writing. I was at home alone that night and as I let my faith dissipate I found myself letting fear creep back into my thoughts.

The next day I saw my girlfriend and I told her that I had discovered one of her guardian angels to be Ezekiel. We did some research and discovered that Jeremiah, my guardian, and Ezekiel, her guardian, were the names of two prophets in the Bible and, apparently, if you go back to older versions of the Bible these two Prophet's books were located side by side. Wow.

My lingering question was that my girlfriend did not pressure me and ask me what was the name of her other guardian angel. She had learned just like me that everyone supposedly has "two" guardian angels, so why she did not ask me the name of the other one was a mystery. All I knew is that she saved me by not asking for the second name that day, because I was not prepared to explain to her that I was "receiving" the name Lucifer.

The next night I decided to clair-write again. Seriously thinking I would "fix this situation", and come up the correct name for her other guardian angel and that last night was just a fluke. That is exactly how our ego can decide to take over. So what happened when I tried? I came up with the exact same two names. However, something even more astounding occurred right then. I had ordered my own birth certificate in the mail, so I could get my exact time of birth (because I had suddenly become very interested in getting a true astrological reading about by natal chart). The birth certificate was laying on the bed right beside me. I suddenly got the urge to pay attention to the detail on the certificate. There right in front of me on my certificate, my mother's middle name is Lucinda and my father's middle name is Lucian. What did I say was my female guardian angels name? Oh, that's right "Lucy". Lucinda, Lucian and Lucy I knew were no coincidences, and this started me back down the path of eliminating my own fears, and learning the name Lucifer actually means Lightbearer and was an original name for the planet Venus.

For anyone unfamiliar with the etymology of "angel", it literally means "Messenger of God." I have read that some religions, such as Christianity and Isalm, are openly known to condemn some Archangels throughout the years and stating that they are so called "fallen angels." I read that Archangel Raguel is one of the angels condemned by some. Amazingly, I had a firsthand experience myself with Archangel Raguel, which was more positive than I could have ever imagined, and it was before I learnt about the power of our own negative thoughts. What happened to me is this, when I had a lot of concern about confronting a difficult situation, I consulted the advice of a friend. This friend prayed to God and asked that Archangel Raguel be with me throughout resolving the situation. She explained to me in her words what this angel is known to preside over. Raguel is known as the Archangel that presides over fairness and justice. It was a material situation that had gotten negative financially with a repair store because I was being charged too much, but they had my belongings held hostage until I paid the enormous fee. There was a language barrier at the store and I had already been spoken to unkindly on the phone. I kid you not, I asked this Angel again for help myself right before I went in the store, my first time asking an Angel to be with me, and I did this with complete **faith** that an Angel was in fact listening to me. Faith I understand is the key. When I calmly confronted the situation in the store, an employee literally followed me to my car and this man, in about his 60-70's, shouted "we love you" as I got in my car to drive away. I drove off with the most unbelievable peace and joy about the situation and found myself thanking an Angel, for the first time. Therefore, when I subsequently read about the churches condemnation of Archangel Raguel, it only took a second to think "well if people are acting unfairly in their daily human lives, what better Angel to condemn to continue 'getting away' with behaving badly than Archangel Raguel, right?" Sorry if I sound so sarcastic, but that is where my mind "goes" sometimes when I am really angry at injustice, and this was over the top for me to comprehend. The minute I read that article about the churches history with the angels, I knew intuitively what I was reading was so wrong. I found myself crying my eyes out and telling Archangel Raguel directly that I loved him, that I knew he was only here to help us and that I was so sorry that we had done that.

Jumping back to reading my own birth certificate that night, and seeing the Lucian, Lucinda and Lucy parallels to Lucifer, I began to do some research. I began to learn immediately about the meaning of Lucifer's name as the "Bearer of Light". I have been told that he was intended to be "the greatest light bearer of all time." I also began some deep meditative thinking, I know inherently there is nothing evil about me and that I have never intentionally set out to hurt anyone in my life, so it felt odd to have all of these inferences or root words related to Lucifer on my own certificate, after the way I was raised to believe it was such a negative name/word. I make lots and lots and lots of human errors. I make plenty of bad decisions, but I am starting to get much more conscious about the consequences of my thoughts, in addition to my actions. I had always been told that angels do not have free will like we do. So if angels were created to be messengers of God and they have no free will, how can an angel fall? I started to contemplate that Lucifer may have been in the Garden of Eden trying to warn Adam and Eve as God's messenger and once they did what was forbidden they needed someone to condemn. Then, I thought, what could make an angel the greatest light bearer of all time. Of course, "saving souls" and bringing them closer to the love of their creator came to mind. Then, I realized that if you were called a name and condemned like "the Devil" or "Satan" and that for centuries people would be sending negative thoughts to you and therefore negative energy directed toward you. I think anyone would agree that would be quite a weight for an angel to bear, especially if they have no free will and were simply fulfilling the plan that their creator had laid out for them. Suddenly a light bulb went off in my head, and I realized that completely made sense that Lucifer has been required to bear the greatest weight of negative thoughts. Intuitively, I drew my own conclusion that a devil does not exist and that hell is what we create with our own thoughts on earth. I no longer believe in fallen angels, makes no sense without free will. Do not get me wrong that I do intuitively sense that with our thoughts and collective consciousness we can pool together enough negative energy to create evil forces and demons that could be really powerful, but I do not feel that there is a devil that is our Creator's equal and direct opposite that used to be an angel created by that same Creator that has infinite knowledge. I believe that our Creator graciously, with Total love, granted humans free will and the ability to also "create" with our thoughts and actions, and we choose when we create negative thoughts.

So now it is time for me to confront this situation head-on and explain all of this new understanding to my girlfriend and tell her the truth about the names of her guardian angels. I tell her how being associated with the name that means "the greatest lightbearer of all time" seems to completely strengthen and reinforce the career that she chose to be a Reiki healer, which is often referred to as a lightworker. I did. She took the knowledge in stride, and I tell you that the truth of this knowledge brought us closer to each other in love and not negativity than I could have ever imagined. It was all my unfounded fear in the first place.

One other unique thing happened while I was discussing this information with her. I had read and been told that feathers are often a sign in life that angels are with you. Well, while we were sitting together there suddenly appeared two white feathers in between us. We looked at each other in disbelief and said in sync "those weren't there a minute ago." I knew where they could have come from, but it was not possible while we were sitting there. We were inside my house, and I do not have a bird.

Subsequent to telling her about the guardian angel names, I had lunch one day at my house for this girlfriend and another girlfriend to get caught up with each other's lives before I took off to Europe for the summer. All of it happened within a very short period of time after I read that National Geographic about the Bible that I mentioned above. I told both of them about my intuition about there not being a devil as an actual entity (only negative energy forces from our own thoughts) and about **women** being written out of "religious" history. Then, I admitted to myself and both of them that I was having a mental struggle with the fact that I was strained with caring for a house by myself at that time and resented the fact that I had to call in **a man** to help me hang the paintings on the wall that I had purchased in Grand Cayman. They both responded at the exact same time, "no you don't." I looked at them, and they said "we know who you need, call Mel." Mel is a **woman** firefighter that has a handyman business on the side. So maybe that energy that I mentioned that I felt earlier about a feminine guardian angel for my Italian friend was a female after all…

So as Mel entered my life and began to help me with many handyman tasks. I began to learn about her spiritual abilities and talents, although she was not initially open to discussing such matters. She felt safer discussing spirituality with me after hearing about my sojourns. She asked if I had ever heard of Kinesiology? I had recently and knew that a lot of people refer to it as muscle testing. She recommended using this talent to choose colors and layouts that were best for me energetically (sort of like Feng Shui, but using your own internal energy). So, my path goes like this with her, while I was standing underneath the now hung Grand Cayman

paintings with her, a book title suddenly jumped out at me visually on my own bookcase beside of us. It was not the most prominent color on the shelf, but like I mentioned, it is all my eyes would allow me to focus on. It is called *True at First Light*.

I had to grab it because, as I have stated, a lot I have been reading has been about the light of our Creators love lately and the Bearer of Light. I had never heard of the book and I just sat it on the table between us, but I do believe that Mel had a lot to do with the energy of drawing it to me. I called an ex-boyfriend to see if the book had been his and if he knew about it. My intuition was right, it was his, and since he knew a bit about my journey to this point, he was very interested in helping me research it. But first, he drew my attention to the fact that the book was written by Ernest Hemingway and he reminded me by saying "Tracy, you know the author of *The Old Man and the Sea*." And I said "What did you just say." Then, I ran to the balcony of my second floor to look at the Guy Harvey paintings from Grand Cayman that Mel had just hung up for me and I was staring at a wall full of fish and two images of the "The Old Man and Sea." I kid you not!!

My ex-boyfriend continued to tell me that the book was written after Hemingway and his fourth wife, Mary, finished one of their safari trips to Africa, and that Hemingway and Mary had been in **two consecutive plane crashes**, different planes two days apart. He said "Hemingway was officially pronounced dead after the second plane crash and woke up reading his own obituaries in the hospital." I said "Wow, I do not know why but apparently, I have to read this book", so I downloaded it on my computer tablet. Now we are ready to take off for the Summer of 2012 and begin that journey.

ST LUCIA AND EUROPE

I first went to St Lucia to begin the summer of 2012. When I was asked by a spiritual healer right before the trip to imagine myself in beautiful place and imagine myself surrounded by our Creator's white light and energy in that place whenever I wanted to get started on a meditation, this was the place I had chosen in my mind to go to. Sitting and staring at the Grand Piton mountains in St Lucia.

Although I had been to St Lucia before, I saw everything with completely different eyes (maybe my "third eye" as they say). I started reading *True at First Light* there in St Lucia. I learnt quickly that Hemingway's style is to write with a lot of inference and reading between the lines. But also I learnt that he was deeply imbedded in African culture and starting a "new religion" in Africa. Much of the book is written in Swahili and I did not realize there was a glossary for a lot of the words until too late. So while in St Lucia I went on a tour with a local tour guide from Soufriere that had amazing knowledge of the history of the lands beside the resort where I was staying as none other than a plantation with a history of a large population of African slaves. It was well known that many escaped or were eventually freed and lived on the island.

Continuing to read **True at First Light**, I had just gotten to the point of understanding that Mary, Hemingway's wife, was going to kill a lion on the safari. The book reads like a documentary of the safari, not a fiction. It is just too real. The book stated that Mary had to kill this lion and had to kill it "clean" or that literally all the tribes in Africa would be impacted. I believe that Hemingway believed this to be true, and he states that his own wife would commit "Suttee" if she did not kill this lion by herself clean. Suttee was not in the dictionary, so one can only assume suicide. It lead me to the local national archive office in St Lucia to get help translating the meaning of Swahili words in my book and to talk spiritually with them about their island country, which gave me a deeper understanding spiritually about the world. The book goes into great detail about Mary's mission and how insane it was driving her, she was painfully aware of her impact on Africa, and she knew this was "**her lion**."

Next, I left for Europe. I thought I was going to a "City" named Cinque Terre. My hotel was actually located in a City called Sestra Levanto, which caused a little confusion for my poor driver that had to get me to the hotel. Cinque Terre is actually the adjacent region consisting of five cities, which the name Cinque Terre translates to five earths. A lot happened here, but what stood out right away in the Cinque Terre region, besides Mother Earth's beauty, was a little art gallery. The art gallery said Luci over the door, so I could not resist it. Luci (pronounced Luche in Italian) meant the artist was the painter of Light, similar to America's Thomas Kinkade, this Italian artist was famous for their techniques related to light. So here we go again, I am reminded that about the Bearer of Light on one of my first days in Europe. There was so much more that happened to me spiritually between Italy and Switzerland (chock full of life lessons) that it had my head in the clouds trying to integrate everything, but the next very strong sign/signal along this particular path happened in Monaco.

I met a new friend in Monte Carlo. I found out through our chance meeting that he was deeply spiritual and had been training under a master. Travelling alone myself and for the most part being on this amazing journey of connections alone it was a relief to be able to quickly share with someone, that even though a stranger, showed no indication of doubt about anything that had occurred to me and was as fascinated as I was to hear each other's journey without judgment.

He was a Leo and so am I, so I was really noticing this lion theme appearing before me in Europe as I continued to read **True at First Light**, about Mary and her lion. He surrounded himself with images of lion's which he believed to spiritually strengthen himself as a Leo. I admitted to him that I had learnt about Archangels just a few months earlier and had felt a strong infinity toward Archangel Ariel. I had seen her image on a book as a protector surrounded by animals, but especially lions that she protected, and she had blonde hair like mine that was braided which reminded me of my Cherokee grandmother. I referred to her and myself as Lionesses jokingly with him. I began to notice and see statues and images of lion's everywhere I went in Europe. Even on my own hotel room door knocker, since when do rooms get their own knocker?

LONDON

After a few more countries, I landed in London in the summer of 2012 right before the Olympics. The first night I went on a walk to find healthy vegan food and found myself diverted and watching a Broadway type production of the movie Ghost (the one Demi Moore and Whoopi Goldberg had performed in a movie). Believe me, did that play ever look different through my eyes at this juncture. When I exited the play, I was still hungry; it was late. I had started trying to use my intuition and kinesis energy to direct me where to go to locations in the countries and had not been disappointed with where it lead yet. I had also been told that Indian restaurants would be good for me since I was trying to stay with a vegan diet while travelling. You really cannot get a larger signal from the universe than a huge red arrow on a sign pointing down and stating "Indian Restaurant." So I started walking toward what I would almost consider an alley because the street is so narrow in downtown London. The street is called **Neal Street**. When I state that once you awaken you may begin to witness a lot of synchronicities, this was a prime example. As I walked down this tiny street, I noticed the Indian restaurant, then a closed vegan restaurant, followed by an organic pharmacy, then an organic soap shop, next a restaurant named Pix. Pix restaurant/bar was actually still open that late. It offered free late hour bar food buffet that had **plenty of vegan** options, like gazpacho in martini glasses and eggplant, etc. As if the universe had directed me straight to Pix, or maybe the whole alley packed with organic options?

When I sat down at Pix, I noticed a devil on the menu that was the symbol for the restaurant and I was taken back for a second and then remembered that I do not believe in a devil and should never think negative thoughts or I will attract negative to myself (google Law of Attraction for more on this). So upon second look and a little time for my brain to translate, the name of Pix translates into the Taurus and it was not a devil, but a picture of the astrology sign of the bull. Then I looked out the window and across the street and there was an astrology shop, so I knew that was my next stop. The shop was closed but I stood there gaping looking in the window. The entire window, **at least 25 items**, was full of lion's. Everything you could ever possibly want to know about a Leo. I was shocked and knew I was coming back here the next day to visit this store when it was open. I continued down this tiny alley/street and there was a psychic crystal shop and another Indian restaurant and I looked back in the dark and wondered if any of the store owners or employees were aware they had all been attracted by the universe to locate together?

I walked back to Neal Street and went to the astrology shop the next day. I received guidance from an employee that confirmed that I should follow up on my intuition to go see the lion at the London zoo while I was in town. Plus, I got the urge while in the shop to buy a small crystal known as **citrine** which I learned while there is known to have a vibration to heal people, but I did not know why I felt compelled to buy it.

OLYMPICS

Meanwhile back in my hotel in London I was still trying to get help to locate tickets to the Olympic games, and more than anything, the opening ceremony. I failed to mention earlier that I had opened my own travel agency and that I had tried everything I could think of for three months straight with all of the help from my peer agents and to no avail had not been able to procure tickets to the games for myself. I thought for sure that I could get help from the concierge at my hotel in London to get these tickets since I arrived several days before the games were to start. However, I quickly discovered the devastating fact that if someone from London sold an American a ticket to the Olympics that was designated for a British resident that person would be fined $25,000 and have a charge for the "offense" placed on their permanent record (hence, the numerous empty seats that many of you saw on television during the games). As soon as I learnt this fact, I had no intention of getting anyone in trouble, but I decided to pray about it again since I felt so intuitively drawn to go to the games. Plus, I had had individuals with psychic abilities tell me before I left Orlando that London was supposed to have something very spiritual happen for me, and I felt very strongly that it was supposed to happen at the games, or why did the universe help me get here at the perfect time, right (I mentioned that I no longer believe in coincidences)? When I say I prayed, I used that kinesis energy skill. I had learnt that the more I practice using this skill the faster the answers come. This time I prayed to discover whether I was in fact intended to attend the Olympic games and I was specific about the opening ceremony. I received a quick and definite "yes." I had also been given a book called **Force vs. Power**. Utilizing the message given to me in that book, I had done my due diligence and taken all responsibility that I knew of to try to procure the tickets to the games myself (which is forcing it to happen), so it was time to completely surrender to our Creator and watch "the Power" instead. I no longer thought or stressed about going, I just knew that I would go if I was supposed to.

A couple days passed and I went to breakfast in my hotel, where I had eaten alone the past several mornings. This morning was special because it was the day of the opening ceremony for the Olympics and my hotel in London was sold out and packed for breakfast. Therefore, we all sat closer together, and I particularly sat by a delightful gentleman. We struck up a conversation while he waited for his significant other to return from the buffet. He asked if I was enjoying myself and what particularly I was doing in London. I stated that "somehow I had found myself on a spiritual journey this summer throughout Europe and had been told that London was supposed to be particularly spiritual for me according to predictions." His ears perked up and I went on to say that "I felt strongly like I was supposed to attend the Olympics games but I knew it was impossible to get tickets, but I had not given up hope yet." What do you know, that couple was from San Francisco and they helped me secure tickets within a couple hours; a legal American ticket for less than what Londoners could purchase them for. How about them apples? So there I was leaving the hotel to scurry off to the ceremony of a lifetime.

I ran into one of the concierge gentlemen that worked at the hotel in the lobby and they could not believe that I had secured an American ticket to the opening ceremony. They were astounded. They mentioned to me that they had just been told that one of the American guests in the hotel was also trying to sell swim tickets for the opening swimming event the very next day. They introduced me to those guests, because they happened to be sitting right in the lobby. It was a lovely family but they let me know that the value of the ticket was $1,000 dollars. I told them that I really appreciated the offer to purchase a ticket, but I could not spend that much for one event. Then I had to run back up to my room because I forgot to take a jacket. All of a sudden there was a knock at my hotel room door. That American family in lobby stopped by and just handed me their ticket for the swimming opening day and said they just did not want it to go to waste! Seriously, I felt like I was floating on a cloud on the way to the ceremony.

At the open ceremony, I kid you not, my last-minute seat was close enough for me to get a picture of Paul McCartney singing on stage with my cell phone. So as we all stood there in the stands and cheered for every single country that walked on to the track, I got the overwhelming feeling of the "energy" of all of the countries representatives being together in one place. I could never explain what that felt like in words, but a bit like electricity running through my body and pressure and wonderful. I did not know why, but I began to cry at the ceremony, and I tried to hide that fact behind my sunglasses. There was a woman from South Africa standing to my left and she was crying also and she placed her hands in a prayer position and bowed to me and I felt compelled to do the same in return. It felt like true love from deep in my heart toward her, and I am telling you that I have never been like this (I had been raised thinking it would show weakness to cry in public). We may never know why we were all crying, but it felt wonderful. Then, I looked up to the sky and said "Thank you so much, please tell me how to give back for this amazing opportunity I have received tonight." As if I was meditating at the ceremony, I had an epiphany and saw everyone around me differently suddenly. There "he was" on millions of shirts, hats and flags surrounding me again. I went for a walk and "he was everywhere." I suddenly realized that Britain's logo for their Olympic team, Team GB, is **the Lion**. He is pictured in graphic form with red and blue flames for his mane. I say "the" lion, because there is only one male lion in the London zoo. After a few more thousand images of the lion passed me, I looked up at heaven and said "I get it", and I knew I was going to go see the lion at the zoo soon.

When the **Queen** arrived at the opening ceremony, she was way on the other side of the Olympic stadium from me. I remember thinking how grateful I was to be there, but I wished I could be close enough to see the Queen once because of the tremendous respect I have for her. I remember I had just read that the Queen is raised from birth with the belief that she is appointed to the throne directly by God, very interesting to me. The next day after the opening ceremony, I headed back to Olympic stadium to use my "free" swim ticket for the first day of the games. Some would say it was just preliminary swimming trials, to determine which competitors even get to compete. However, I got see Locke and Phelps swim side by side and get a photo of them. I got to see Ms. Dana Vollmer break a World Record right in front of my eyes, unbelievable

experience. Then, the unimaginable happened. I heard a loud shuffle and people started jumping over the extremely steep bleachers with their cameras in hand to my left. And there she was, with her amazing royal hand waving right in my direction with her regal blue suit and matching hat, the Queen of England. I had been seeing 111 a lot on clocks and signs and license plates, etc. I had to come to understand the significance of the number meant to carefully monitor your thoughts, because everything you are thinking is manifesting rapidly; whether you are thinking positive or negative thoughts. It sure seemed as if my every desire was manifesting immediately.

But there was still that **lion** on all those flags, shirts, banners and hats looking at me on this second day of the Olympics at the swimming opening event. I said again to heaven "I'm going, I'm going."

FAMILY LESSONS

There is one more thing of significance I must go back in time to say before I can go on. My aunt suffered an aneurism early in 2012 before I went to Europe. I had been recommended a book called Healing with the Angels, that I happened to have with me when the aneurism struck, and I went to visit my Aunt. What I learnt a lot about from this tragic family incident was about Archangel Raphael the **"green healing rays" of light** that many have seen during healing miracles. The doctors said that my Aunt had no chance of survival and sent her home to family to essentially pass away.

More than one year later, with a lot of prayers from family (the book taught special prayers I said), that Aunt is still around and smiling. She is one of the few people on earth that has graduated from Hospice.

Another family lesson I learnt was about a grandmother that passed away before I was born. My Mom told me a specific story repeatedly as a child about her and it stuck in my memory. Mom said that when she was with her mother at her death bed, my Grandmother looked in her the eyes and said "honey what are crying about, don't you see all of the Angels here in the room surrounding us?" I do not remember a lot from childhood, but I can tell you I am glad that one was repeated enough to stick in. Then I saw a picture of that grandmother and went, huh? My Mom and I are both blonde hair and blue eyes. This woman had dark looking skin and jet black hair with a really square jaw. Mom let me know she was half Swedish (obviously what we got), but also half Cherokee Indian. This particular Aunt with the aneurism looked the most like the Cherokee side of any of my mother's seven siblings. So on my most recent visit to my Aunt, my cousins told me they walked into the room where she was lying in bed to check on her (she can barely talk now except a whisper, but thank God no coma, which is an unbelievable miracle with that size aneurism) and my Aunt was wide awake just staring strangely at the ceiling. They looked up and said "Granny what are you looking at." It was a plain white ceiling. She said "Jesus." I said "do not ever doubt what she says she sees" and told them about their great grandmothers' **clairvoyance** seeing all the angels right before she passed.

THE ZOO AND THE LION

Now it was time and I knew I needed to take a day and visit the lion in the zoo, before I go crazy with images of lions everywhere, on huge statues, buildings, everywhere. So I caught "the tube" (London's subway) over to the zoo. The marketing for the Zoo during the Olympics was almost non-existent. Considering this was London, I was dumbstruck to see how insipid the entrance to the zoo was. I actually tried two entrances along the huge perimeter boundary before I was able to figure out where they let the public enter the Zoo. I went into the gift shop at the entrance of the zoo and there was nothing really special about the lion exhibit in the store, or anything for me to read about the lion family before I walked on to the exhibit itself. In other major cities, for example DC, I have seen entire gift shop buildings dedicated to one animal, such as, lions. It was abundantly clear to me that the marketing for these animals was underfunded.

I walked along the path to the lion's area mumbling the whole way to the universe that I was going to "get this over with, but I do not have time for this and cannot stop to see all of the other animals right now", because for heaven's sake I have tickets to more Olympic games, right? In particular, I scored tickets to the US Men's basketball the next night. I am a huge NBA fan. After I also started to see the number "111" popping up everywhere (synchronicities), it seemed I started having the opportunity to get tickets to any event I thought I want to attend.

As mentioned in Part I, the London Zoo has been around since the eighteenth century and over the years, due to lack of funding, some of the facilities have begun to fall into disrepair due to their age. In addition, some were built too small in the first place, but have become utterly undersized due to the successful breeding and expansion of animal families. When I got to the Lion's area, I was appalled. There was a chalk board drawing that explained that the Zoo tries to maintain the habitat for the lions to replicate their true natural environment in the wild. Therefore, the chalk board explained that the lions are fed blood ice cubes. What the heck? What kind of inappropriate message is this to tell children? What are the children supposed to grow up to think the African and Asian natives run around with pink ice cubes and ice tea? Then it gets worse, huge letters that state "born to kill." Again, is this the best message we can give children about this regal "King of the Beasts" that is the Olympic logo for Great Britain? As I mentioned in Part I, the moat of water around the lion's area is completely consumed by disgusting green swamp water, and you know animals have better instinct than we do to stay away from polluted water unless they are desperate. The funding for maintenance was the desperate situation, the outdoor space for the lions has not been maintained in so long that there is trash on the grounds and the lawn was not mowed. I have photos of these conditions in Part I.

Therefore, the lions are kept inside in this little dirt area surrounded by concrete and glass that children are allowed to walk right up to and bang on the glass all day long. And believe me they banged on the glass. In case you are not aware, lions in the wild are supposed to sleep an enormous amount of hours each day for their health (think about a house cat). It gets worse. This concrete and glass area is the size of a family living room in a regular house and it is not just the lion (which remember is the symbol of the Olympics for London) but it is also two Lionesses AND **two brand new lion cubs**. Yes, in this same small space. Great Britain has the most beautiful rare and endangered lion family right here in London with no space to roam.

I took a photo of the two beautiful cubs when they were sitting side by side. You can see that the five lions are trapped in the tiny space of concrete walls. Then I looked down at the photo I had taken. I could not believe my eyes. I had actually photographed this **"green healing ray" of light** that I had read about (refer to the inset box above about *Family Lessons*). The green ray coming from the sky was directly over the heads of the two cubs, but not over anything else. I

have attached the photo below (many of you are aware that what appeared on the screen of my iPhone would not look the same when it was blown up for this book publication, so I asked the publisher to do the best they could to make it look the same for readers as how it appeared to me, but I tell you even more about the photos authenticity later). I have read that Archangel Raphael who is listed in spiritual documents of many religions utilizes a green ray/energy for healing and apparently that is why hospitals have predominantly green walls (not sure if it explains the green choice for jello too…)

I walked to the bench across from their habitat and put on my sunglasses and sat there and cried and told our Creator that "I completely understand, and I know I am supposed to do something," but I asked "how, what do I do?" I felt helpless. I sat there and reflected on a memory that surfaced from my childhood (see insert box).

Then a young girl came up and sat down on the bench beside me in the London Zoo and she started crying too. Our Creator really does

> When I was about 10 years old my mother took me to a zoo that had a tiger in a round cage in Roanoke, Virginia. The entire cage was the size of a bathroom and the tiger just paced in a circle. It was supposed to be such a beautiful outing with Mom and I left totally despondent, as a child knowing how sickeningly wrong it was to trap and hold a beautiful creature like this for our viewing pleasure. But I left that zoo years ago, thinking that it was a cruel world and there was nothing we could do about it. Now that tiger is no longer alive.

know how to activate that instinct in me to take care of others. Once you show me an animal family in jeopardy and now a child both in need, I am suddenly no longer helpless, protection courage builds inside me quickly and not a lot can stop me from doing something to change a situation once this develops inside me. I asked the young girl if she was alright and assumed she was crying about the same thing I had seen. She said "no" (indicating she was not alright), and I asked if she had parents at the zoo. She indicated yes and that they were walking around. She went on to tell me that she did not feel well. Suddenly, I felt something in my pocket, the **citrine** crystal that I had strangely had the intuition to purchase at the astrology shop seemed to have a purpose, right? Do know how many crystals there are in the world, why would this be the only little one in my pocket at the zoo and why did I take it with me to the zoo? I handed it to her and told her it was a special crystal that had been used throughout history to heal people. By the time her parents came she was just sitting there looking at the crystal smiling. And me? My inner Lioness was totally empowered now.

I saw a female groundskeeper coming my way and stood up off the bench and asked, sort of politely (I hope), why the lion's water looked the way it did. She said not to worry that it was on a rotation schedule and gets cleaned in cycles. I looked her right in the eye's and said "with all due respect, the Olympics are going on in London, this is the London zoo, if there was ever money to clean this water, you and I both know it would have been done by now for this huge event." I went on to say "I am not looking to blame, I know the zoo obviously does not have money for maintenance, you need help, I want to help financially, who do I talk to?" She said "come with me and we can go see if I can introduce you to someone." What are the chances that the Development Director for the zoo would be there at lunch time and available on the second day of the Olympics? That is what happened, he came right out and shook my hand and I told him that I wanted to know what the situation was and he explained they were doing a new exhibit for the tigers this year, and as a result could give more land to the lions at some point in the future. However, there were no plans right then and even no drawings of a design yet for this, and more importantly, no funding for the design or the construction.

I had never been this inspired in my life to right a wrong. I knew doing nothing would haunt me, but getting involved would make me feel alive. Can you imagine feeling so convinced after the entire summer of synchronicities to this lion that the whole universe had directed you to this point and time and now handed the decision over to your "free will." What was I going to do?

I told the zoo's Development Director that I was going to start a campaign right now during the Olympics and hand out fliers. I told him that if the Zoo or City of London would help raise funds I would match the first $25,000 dollar for dollar. Now, it is no one's business what I do or do not have, but I do not have $25,000 laying around to spare, and I am responsible as the financial power of attorney to take care of my mother who is in an assisted living facility. But I honestly felt like I would not have a reason to live if I did not make this offer. I felt like everything had happened in my life to lead to this moment. I knew the zoo would need a lot more money than what I offered and even the match.

The zoo Development Director was a nice gentleman, and he said I can see you are very emotional about the lion, but I really think you should think about this for a night because it is a huge commitment. I told him "no, that my mind was made up and I was going to spend the rest of the time with the events that I have tickets to go see to solicit contributions to the zoo for the lion habitat rehabilitation." The Director looked at me and said "Lucifer is really going to appreciate this." I took a few steps backwards, and tried to catch my breath. I said "what did you say?" He said "didn't anyone tell you that Lucifer is the lion's name?" …………..he said Lucifer was the lion's name. Dear Lord, there it was, everything coming full circle

Following spiritual signs lead me to my path of destiny that eventually took me to this lion and beyond into life full speed ahead.

right before my eyes. My whole purpose laid out right in front of me. I was on fire. I stood right there in front of the Director with my giant sunglasses on and bawled my eyes out with a smile on my face.

Mary had her lion in Hemingway's biography and this is the path that took me to **my Lion**, Lucifer, the lightbearer. I feel like my heart is energetically connected to his. I feel responsible for him. I do not have the money to help him alone, but I feel like the universe is behind me and I do not feel powerless. I feel like one person can make a difference. As I sit here crying writing this, if my path helps Lucifer and his family, I will know what true Joy feels like. I fell in love with him as soon as I saw him; he let his cub come up and lick his face and then he rolled over and cleaned his face with his huge paws.

CAMPAIGN

So I went straight back to my hotel in London and wrote a campaign letter to raise money for this amazingly beautiful lion family. At first, I did a knee jerk reaction, and let my anger out and almost attacked Londoners for the situation. I love Londoner's and knew I was making a huge mistake. Everyone that I spoke to on the way back to the hotel about the situation had known nothing about the conditions, had not been to the zoo on over 20 years and they all were completely empathetic with the situation and wished me the best with the campaign. So I straightened up my act and re-wrote the campaign with love and not anger. I explained to readers that this was a public facility and that we were all responsible for it. Please remember what I wrote in Part I, the lion does not recognize country boundaries, he just needs help. I spoke with the Director at the zoo, and he anticipated needing about $5 million Euro to build a really nice habitat for the lion family. What is most frustrating to discover is that if every Londoner knew about the need and decided to give only one Euro the entire problem would be more than solved (there are 7 million population in London alone), or spread throughout England and around the world, less than a penny needed. But there was no project and no one was even asking.

For the campaign, I had to keep borrowing the hotel's computers at the concierge desk late that night to finish typing it, because I only had a little computer tablet with me. The hotel was more than accommodating and after they learned of my campaign and spiritual journey, they disclosed to me the spiritual history of the hotel itself, go figure (where else would I end up lodging).

The next afternoon I finished editing the campaign flyer and attaching my photographs into the campaign and got it printed. I headed into the hotel's lounge bar to grab a bite to eat, watch the games on the large screen TV and figure out my plan for distribution at the men's US Olympic basketball game that night, which of course meant I was quietly praying for inspiration because I had no idea how to do this distribution to enough people.

I saw a unique man in a turban sitting between me and the television screen. I smiled politely at him. He saw the concierge desk bring me the flyers when they were done printing hot off the press and how I was greeted by the hotel staff, because they all knew about my mission at that point and my donation to the zoo. The man asked what I doing, and I said I had just started a campaign to save the Lion in the London zoo. He said tell me more about that and I handed him my flyer. He looked at me and said "you have no idea, you are one lucky lady." I looked at him and said "I do not believe in luck." He told me that he was helping build schools in Africa through his connections to the Sikh religion and that if I could stay that he would talk to me after his business meeting about how to get the funds I needed to raise for the lion. I walked back up the concierge desk and said "I have more good news and some bad news for me." I said "I think I maybe raised the $5 million Euro that I need for the lion, but unfortunately I have to stay here tonight and miss the basketball game, because now I am the lion's Ambassador. I picked their chins up off the floor and gifted my Olympic ticket to one of them that was getting off work." I became great friends with my new campaign companion, Mr. Sangha, and he told me of a story about a gentleman named Lord Paul that once had a daughter that loved animals in that particular zoo. He said Lord Paul was a gracious man and had not only donated to the London Zoo in the past, but that there was a statue of his daughter in that zoo (if I had to guess, I would say her energy was still around doing good to help that zoo by bringing us all together, but that's my speculation). He said he would do what he could to help me get this information to Lord Paul and seemed quite sure that he may be able to get more help as well. However, I know that a lion's life span is not long enough to wait for these potentials and that I had to keep trying to raise the funds. Can you imagine if I waited on the zoo, City and royal bureaucracy for approval of the campaign flyer for me to hand out for the Olympics (they cannot help their red tape, it is done to protect us from lawsuits or disgrace)? But privately I could move right ahead with my flier. I guess that is why a Leo was chosen for this project; just do it.

SINCE LEAVING EUROPE

My first stop was NAPA. I went to a charity event (V Foundation) for cancer in Jimmy Valvano's honor. That is where I ran into an ESPN photographer. As you can imagine, the experts are pretty sharp with camera details once they make it to the level of an ESPN professional (walking around with his foot and half long lens). I said "hey, can you take a look at this picture I took of some cubs in a zoo in London and tell me what that 'green ray of light' is over their heads." Now, this was one confident individual. They need the ego for the job that they do, and I am sure he is excellent at it. He responded quickly "oh that's a lens flare (don't quote me on what he called it, I'm not a photographer), and I could reproduce that." He proceeded to let me know that "I didn't realize who I was talking to here." He let me know that he is often called upon as an expert witness in court cases to tear apart people's fraudulent images. Obviously, it did not phase me since

I have nothing to hide and figured I was about to learn a lesson that would be useful someday. He said "if I was testifying I could tear you apart, because I would know that you took the picture with that iPhone and therefore, I would know the day, the minute you took it, the GPS coordinate where you were standing, the angle of the sun on that day, and he said I could repeat that lens flare." I was like "cool, how would you repeat it?" He said you would have to be standing facing the cubs and that and the sun would have to just hit you from behind like this. Then I proceeded to show him in the picture the little glimpse of the stone/concrete roof that I was standing under when I took the picture and the picture that I had taken less than one minute before of the same spot with no green ray. The cubs had moved over to that spot together after I took the first picture. Then he scratched his head and said "I don't know, never seen anything like that." I said "cool, thanks." I knew he had just validated the authenticity of that amazing photo, which I needed as a non-photographer.

Afterwards, I flew back to DC, to visit my Mom, and took her to a beauty shop on King Street. While in the beauty shop, technicians started talking to me about spiritually related issues when I asked for products without chemicals (sticking to my vegan regime even for my hair), so I proceeded to tell them about the lion mission and how excited I was. The next thing I knew, a gentleman came up to me in the salon and said if you can write this up, I know the gentleman that owns Virgin Airlines and maybe I can help you raise funds for the lion. Plus, I discovered that my male hair dresser was an inventor and had designed an alternative energy source that could run electricity for an entire City with no maintenance costs for a decade and no industrial waste to construct (I should mention that my design firm was focused on city planning, so this is extremely significant for me both spiritually and materially). So, I started introducing him to organizations that support alternative energy for jurisdictions. Last but not least, I discovered that he has a home in **Cyprus** right where I was considering attending a spiritual workshop that I had just been told about. The workshop teaches meditation by the daughter of "Spyros Sathi" the mystic and renown healer described in an international book as the "Magus of Strovolos". I had made so many spiritual connections in this one salon visit alone, my head was ready to explode. I did not even know this salon existed before this day.

You might be wondering how I discovered the about the workshops in Cyprus? I had felt drawn spiritually to attend my high school reunion while I was in DC. I had so much going on with just returning from overseas and taking care of my Mom's needs, that I would normally be inclined to skip the invite to the reunion, but again I felt strongly that there was a purpose for me to be there. The day of the reunion started out rather unique, I received some information from a close friend that had made me unusually emotional. So I was further fighting the urge to go to the event, because I did not feel like socializing. My high school girlfriend wanted me to go with her and I prayed and kept getting a strong intuition saying "yes" to attend. At the reunion, I saw everyone from such a new perspective. I saw so many people stuck and dwelling mentally on bad things that had happened to them in the past, even as far back as high school. These individuals were, therefore, still letting those past actions and occurrences impact their future by hanging on to all that negative energy. Well, I have to say I thought the reunion itself was uneventful that ended abruptly at 11:00 pm, sort of a real downer after the somber morning I had already experienced. The reunion was held on a military base in DC. My girlfriend and I had decided to get a hotel room to share on the base so there would be zero drinking and driving. I was praying inside and asking the universe why in the world had my intuition pushed me to come to this event, it seemed so unnecessary considering the amazing path I had been following throughout the summer. Back at the hotel on the base, many friends started to gather in the lobby to hang out after the event. Because of my emotions about the somber morning, the embarrassment of a non-eventful reunion (that's my awful "Leo pride" coming through), and the fact that I had a room to stay in with a girlfriend, I felt I made a poor choice for the night. I know that alcohol weights me down and is not something that anyone should include in their life when they are experiencing emotions that are more on the depressed side of the psyche. More important, I had recently learned through friends that alcohol can disconnect a person spiritually; it has even been written about to open doors for psychic attacks. However, in that instance I decided to completely let my guard down and drink; I was essentially "giving up" but felt I had nothing to lose. You could not buy alcohol in the military hotel, which the majority of us did not know until we were already there, but some friends did know and planned ahead by bringing some personal alcohol. I was standing beside one of my biggest nemesis back in high school. When we were young, we used to argue and antagonize each other intensely in class. I was curious to see if he was the same and if he would recognize the change in me spiritually and that he would not be able to get negative responses from me like when I was a tightly wound ball of 11th grade fury. I was preparing myself to find the "lesson" or love in every comment that came from him, even if it did not seem like a positive comment.

But here at the reunion, I was the one to receive the encouraging gift from him, he had nothing to say but positive things about life past, present and future….and because I am female, of course, I was the only one of the two of us being offered free, difficult to obtain alcohol (the event was "BYOB"). I was given two bottles, so I offered one to my friend. He thanked me, declined and quipped that he generally avoids alcohol, because he feels that "it obstructs [his] spiritual sensitivity." "Is that not the biggest 'kick in the pants' the universe could have given me?" I thought, to get me to set the alcohol down. I said "What did you say?" He proceeded to share some of his experiences over the past six years, along with wonderful reading materials about spirituality, meditation, healing, numerology, etc. I had not expected having someone that could even remotely relate to at the reunion about the energies I had started feeling and the synchronicities I had been experiencing. To date, I have not caught up to the half of his reading recommendations. He introduced me to the healers that offer the workshops in **Cyprus**. As they say, the universe will provide guides/teachers when the time is right, and I could not have been more open and ready for the knowledge.

Finally, I flew back home to Florida. Right away, I went to a wonderful lunch party with a group of girlfriends that I have never talked to about my new spiritually. I met 90 percent of these girls that year, when my college roommate invited me to go on a trip to New York with all of them. Two of the girls started whispering about this amazing encounter they had experienced with a psychic they visited, and that one of the girls was positive that the spirit of her father had come to visit her through this psychic. When she said the psychic was a Caucasian American woman working from her house in the suburbs, but that the psychic was able to relay Vietnamese words suddenly, I could tell this girlfriend believed with all of her heart that her father had spoken to her from heaven. Not necessarily in complete sentences, but key Vietnamese words that had significance only for my girlfriend, even the psychic did not know the significance of the words she was "channeling". Amazing, how could anyone contest a psychic that can suddenly speak a language they have never been exposed to? So I opened up about my lion synchronicities and when I started explaining about this tiny alley, a girl in the group chimed in and said "oh, that sounds like **Neal Street**." London is not a small place, I was dumbstruck; this was a tiny alley and I did not even know the specific names of the stores without receipts or bank statements

There are people that have and would recommend to me that I keep anything unique, spiritual or paranormal that I experience to myself, to be quiet – they are "protecting" me, insinuating that people will think I am insane. Well, let me share from personal experience, telling everyone I love and even strangers I meet all about these experiences has brought me closer to my friends and new friends than I could have ever dreamed. I would never trade the love I have felt from sharing. We are all starving for spiritual love in our hearts, and we are starving to HEAR about the hope out there. So please, I implore you, share your experiences with those you love, so many go unmentioned and hidden that could change the world we live in. The days of persecution are behind us. If you are in a job that will not tolerate hearing about love and synchronicities, ask yourself if it isn't your own unfounded fear blocking you from sharing? If you did get a negative reaction, ask yourself what you are doing working there and ask the universe to help you find a more positive environment.

in front of me. Wow. Then my college roommate followed me to my car, and showed tremendous gratitude and relief for being able to relate to me about all these new spiritual adventures. So now my high school and college had followed me right along these steps; there are no coincidences.

Next, a favorite restaurant of mine in Orlando relocated closer to where I live. I had gone a couple times in a row. I did not pay enough attention to the new decorations, I was just always drawn to sit in the same spot. Well I finally focused and realized I was being drawn to sit in front of this really "odd" oil painting on black velvet (think about the antique Elvis-type paintings) with a wooden border that did not match any other theme or decoration in the restaurant. It was an image of the *Old Man and the Sea*. I just sat there with my mouth open and started looking around trying to figure out if this was some sort of message. Here was Hemingway starting up again, but I am back home now. I asked the waitresses what the story was with that particular painting and why it looked so different from the other artwork. Several of the staff said they had no idea, they thought it was just a gift the owner received, but they thought it was really odd to. It caused a very talkative couple to strike-up a conversation with me. I had my laptop in the restaurant and I was staring at some amazing pictures

that my girlfriend had sent to me right when the conversation started. I asked them if they wanted to see some of these amazing shots from around the world, and of course they said yes. Then, one of the waitresses heard me say "now here is my favorite". It was of an older woman standing at the cage of a lion, named Jupiter, and the lion's paws were out through the cage on her shoulders and the two of them were kissing.

The waitress said "oh I want to see that image." Then she exclaims "oh that's nothing, have you seen the YouTube of "**Christian the Lion**." Of course, she has my full attention now. I said "can I pull it up online now", and she said "sure go on our Wi-Fi and watch this it will blow your mind." I did. I am not going to tell you what I saw because it is in your best interest to YouTube it for yourself without any distractions and read the subtitles, and also YouTube search "man hugging lions." All I am going to say is that she came over to me and hugged me and she said "I did not mean to make you cry", and indicated that it was sweet that I felt so much emotion for the compelling story she just shared. I looked at her and smiled and said "I think you just may have helped me save **my lion**."

I knew right then that it was time for me to start writing this book. Thank you *Old Man and the Sea* for attracting me to that particular seat. I hope everyone will be able to witness through my synchronicities all of the remarkable connections that were drawn for me to lead me along this path. It just took the belief in my prayers and consistently asking for guidance while remaining aware. But this was just the first set of synchronicities, see Part III to see how the universe helped me put the plan of action in motion.

A NEW BEGINNING

I mentioned a couple times earlier that I had become a vegan right before I left for Europe, and I want to share with you the path that it took me down. I wish I could say I did it in the beginning from a pure heart to stop the torture and abuse of animals. However, it was a more selfish reason than that, but we are nothing without maintaining our integrity and honesty, so I want to tell you the real reason I altered my diet. I did it because I was intuitively drawn to watch a documentary called *Forks over Knives*, after I had heard the name repeated several times in very different settings (synchronicity at its best). I watched the documentary right after the "terrible three" events occurred in my life that I mentioned earlier. So this new knowledge came to me very early on, before many of these spiritual synchronicities had started to be apparent to me. Looking back, I feel it was as if the universe obviously knew that with my more scientific and mathematical inclined mind that I would need some hard facts to convince me to change. Well that documentary explains how research by American and Chinese (a 70 year study in China) governments had proven that "if you have cancer cells growing in your body, then animal protein will make them grow faster." Proven fact; it is that simple. Guess who has already experienced skin cancer? That is right, me. Guess who has had every member of

I want to lay down for the record what kind of eater I was and what my diet consisted of prior to making these healthy changes. I had a hard working mother that had to support raising me by herself, so going through drive through establishments became a normal occurrence in my life since a very young age. I remember in college, ranking which drinks had the most caffeine on a scale (now the world markets this information in front of us) with my best friends to pull "all-nighters". As an adult, I choose career over health. My patterns included cramming coffee down my throat at the office with no breakfast, followed by soft drinks to stay alert through meetings throughout the day (maybe no lunch unless there was a lunch meeting) and lastly, many times a drive through cheeseburger before I had night meetings, then whatever junk food I wanted at night before bed. I know; it was really bad. As I began to make money, I treated myself to steak that we could not afford in my childhood and I began to crave the meat and anything made with caffeine or sugar.

After changing to vegan and stopping caffeine, I started waking up without that fogginess in my head and this natural energy that I had never experienced before. Plus, may I add, that I went down six dress their immediate family either survive, or like my dad and brother, die from this disease? You got it, me.

In addition, in the Hemingway novel, *True at First Light*, that I have described a little to you, everyone got sick that ate the meat from the lion that had not been killed "with a clean shot." To my new found "spiritual perception", it was because they were eating bad karma, which, of course, I had just started reading a ton about karma. The meat that I had eaten most of my life, probably not only had really bad karma (I'm sure from the way the animals are treated and killed), but has been full of chemicals, metals, you name it. So anyway, thank goodness I was not too stubborn or stupid to start on this new lifestyle. I do like life a lot, so it was time to give this vegetarian thing a try. Well, it was amazing how easy it was to eat vegetarian once I set my mind to it, and within two months I felt so good, I decided to give a vegan diet a try. After all, the documentary had made it clear that it was not only meat, but animal protein, which is dairy, cheese and eggs, etc. which causes the cancer cells to grow faster.

It is not hard to eat vegan. It is simply a choice. I had no problem eating vegan the whole summer in every country in Europe, that's what drew me to the alley called **Neal Street** in the first place. I could name twelve restaurants,

sizes, in less than one year, back to my college size!

Since then I have several people curious about my diet state to me "that it was nice that my skin looked good and that I looked better and had lost amazing weight, but that they could never do what I had done." Well, that is what I thought before too. I had many times at least said to myself that "it would be impossible for me to stop craving meat and sugar or drinking caffeine." I even believed like many "nay-sayers" that it was hard to find or make vegan meals and that I would not have time. Plus, I had heard the same bologna that being vegan was unhealthy and that you would not get enough protein. I do not aim to talk anyone into becoming vegan, and that is <u>not</u> my intent. However, I do think it is critical to alleviate some of these misconceptions:

1. If you are on a budget, and you typically cook at home, there are more vegan recipes available on the internet than you can cook in a lifetime. If you cannot cook worth a flip, like me, stay tuned.

2. I have met some of the most muscular body builders you could imagine that have been vegan for

including bakeries, right now in my home city, Orlando, within a few miles of my house that cater to vegans. I travel a lot. If I visit where there are not restaurants catering to vegans, I find all the soups, cooked side vegetables, potatoes and salads I can eat, even if I dine in a small town. I had a friend tell me "there were no vegan options in their town", so I had them

> Many of the great spiritual thinkers and philosophers went vegetarian/ vegan during their lifetime, including Gandhi, Buddha, Pythagoras, Plato, Leonardo da Vinci, Voltaire, Tolstoy, Einstein and Abraham Lincoln.

walk with me down one commercial street and I pointed out the multitude of choices on the menu. Just the one street I found over 8 restaurants in her town that have specific items on the menu. Plus, if you ask, they will almost always make something special for you, which may mean that you are getting the freshest item on the menu.

Another synchronicity happened, this one pretty funny while I was taking care of my mother, I needed to go out for an evening for work. She has Alzheimer's disease so I needed to get her **a sitter** while I was away. Based upon extensive medical research, I had been feeding my mother really high quality foods

years. If you need proof, checkout www.trinityfitnessllc.com (also, if you are a tough guy, and need to know this is not a wimpy choice, this is a good website for you too).

3. Let me explain the unhealthy issue – if you go vegan and decide to eat only sugar, white bread and black coffee you will probably die soon right? Just like if you were non-vegan and decided to eat only sugar, white bread and black coffee. You still have to eat your veggies and protein, like any healthy diet.

4. As a vegan, I have vegan pizza, lasagna, burritos, hamburgers, quinoa, pasta, granola, oatmeal, bread, cheese (usually almond or coconut milk), yogurt (coconut milk), mayonnaise, butter, sour cream, crackers, chips, soups, hummus, guacamole, salsa, cake, brownies, cookies and sorbet. I cannot begin to name all of the options (try www.vegan outreach. com). Of course, I also have all of the salad, vegetables and fruit I want (even vegan ranch dressing).

5. As for protein and iron, who started the lie that you cannot get protein or iron from veggies? Broccoli and Kale

and supplements to try to detox her brain. For both of us, I stopped using a microwave. Partly due to the research of health hazards I had read and also due to some deeply moving spiritual reading that made me recognize the detriment it could cause to our spiritual connection. But most of all, I stopped using a microwave, due to my own intuition. Many nutritionists agree that it is important to not overcook the nutrients out of food, then how can "nuking" it leave any quality in the food from the earth, let alone processed foods. So this sitter was given specific instructions that my Mom had already had dinner but she could have all of the fruits, nuts, chips and coconut ice cream that she wanted. I thought I had everything bad out of my house now. But I forgot about popcorn, which is fine for a vegan with special butter, and I have a special popper for it. The sitter decided to microwave it. Well, when I got home, the sitter looked like she was in tears. She said she had terrible news for me. She had

6. have more per gram than Beef with NO cholesterol and virtually no fat (check out www.healthaliciousness.com and www.drfuhrman.com). Also for protein (and for those of you that need things to still look like burgers, hotdogs, meatballs and pepperoni), there are many alternatives that have a similar consistency as meat with protein such as seitan, chickun, tofurkey, and tofu. You have to go about two months to stop the cravings for the crap you have put in your body. It is simply a problem with our childhood programming.
7. Some think it will cost more. Isn't meat almost always the most expensive item you put in the grocery cart?

melted my microwave. I realized what had happened and just started laughing. Thank you universe for having my back on that one, right? Now, no one wants a broken item in their house and this one is built in, but I had already wanted to switch it out for another oven, so she was just moving me along.

One of the most delightful messages that I received from the universe, was while I was taking care of my mother and writing this book. I felt like it was a sign to keep me on this path to finish the book. Her Alzheimer's is pretty severe and I had to learn ways to entertain her so I could attempt to get normal household chores done. I had been reading a lot about how releasing blocked creativity could possibly help with healing her brain patterns. I decided to put a blank white canvas in front of her on a small easel, pour her some paint, hand her some pictures and get out of the way to see what she did. She drew and painted the image below in less than one hour. Now, this is a woman in her eighties that has never been a painter in her life and has suffered this prolonged disease for more than a decade. I do not even think I could do what she did in an hour, but that is my own blockage. I was blown away that she sketched a lion and completely painted it in. Of course, her version was not behind bars. When it was time for me to take her home after our extended visit, I told her Assisted Living Facility staff that painting would be really good for her and showed them what she had accomplished. They said the US government would not allow it in the facility; it is a liability. This brought up another profound issue that we all need to tackle together and approach through love – Assisted Living Facilities, unless we figure out a cure for the disease before we all end up like that. Scientists are quickly determining that it is diet related (sugar and metal detox are the most important). I saw great improvement with her memory, based upon the new diet we tried, within a few weeks, but I cannot control the diet at the facility.

ANIMALS AND LION MEAT

I want to discuss what I learnt and was shown along this path about how the animals are treated that become our food. We have drifted a long way from our ancient ancestors. They used to hunt for their food and then bless the animal's body. They were grateful from their hearts for the nourishment it was providing to their bodies. Most Americans are not even sincere about a blessing on Thanksgiving, because they are so far removed from the earth and any true connections to animals.

Many websites and statistics will tell you that over 150 billion (that was billion) animals are slaughtered **each year** for human consumption. As soon as you read these sites, you quickly understand that it is a gross underestimation of the actual numbers. What we are never exposed to is what life is like in the modern agricultural industry and we want to pretend we are not the cause of the abuse that occurs. When I read some of the horrors that are occurring daily on dairy farms it is disgraceful. Below is a quote from www. evolvecampaigns.org.uk:

> "The very saddest sound in all my memory was burned into my awareness at age five on my uncle's dairy farm in Wisconsin. A cow had given birth to a beautiful male calf. The mother was allowed to nurse her calf but for a single night. On the second day after birth, my uncle took the calf from the mother and placed him in the veal pen in the barn - only ten yards away, in plain view of the mother. The mother cow could see her infant, smell him, hear him, but could not touch him, comfort him, or nurse him. The heartrending bellows that she poured forth - minute after minute, hour after hour, for five long days - were excruciating to listen to. They are the most poignant and painful auditory memories I carry in my brain." Dr. Michael Klaper

Many people around the world also discovered that chickens and chicks receive excruciating torture, and therefore, "free range" was recently born. It is amazing for me to witness in stores, how much like androids we have become, to watch people buy free range because it is "popular to do now." They have no idea how the animals were mistreated prior to cage free, they think it is just nutritionally safer for them. Just consider this, even with "cage free" egg purchases - the male chicks are considered worthless. Therefore, at one-day old the male newborns are separated from their sisters, put on a conveyer and either gassed, suffocated or ground up alive. That is what is happening **today**, still, for videos of this go to the website I listed above. In addition, many of the cookies, pies, muffins and bread are made from "battery cage" hens, which is one of the cruelest methods ever invented. If you saw what these animals look like that are even labeled as "cage free", you would understand why we all started to get so much disease from our foods.

Can you imagine how many animals would be saved if we even just agreed to be vegan **one day a week**. There are an estimated 3,000 animals killed to feed us during our lifetimes. After what I have learned, I truly believe if these animals are mistreated and food is not blessed, that the negative karma absorbs right into our bodies. Until the world changes and everything is truly free range without devastating lifestyles for the animals or free of chemicals and metals…. how can we afford not to take care of ourselves?

As I was learning how rare and endangered the Asiatic and African lions were, I became horrified at some new information. **In recent years, lion meat has begun to show up on restaurant menus in the US!** There are currently no USDA rules for how lions are raised or slaughtered in the US. The organization BornFreeUSA reports them on menus in New York, Wichita, Philadelphia, Sacramento, Tucson and Mesa. The population of African lions has already been reduced in half since 1950 and as I mentioned there are only about 400 Asiatic lions left in the wild. Unless we stop some of this madness, lions are going to become extinct.

PART III

ACCOMPLISHMENTS WITH SPIRITUAL SUPPORT

It has been one year since I attended the Olympics and met this precious lion family, so I want to share with you about the amazing progress that has occurred in that timeframe. My support from the universe and the signs and synchronicities surrounding this lion family have not slowed down in the slightest for me, so I will discuss an account of some of what has occurred a little later in this part, particularly under the section titled *Return Visit to London*.

You would think that after everything that happened to me that I wrote about in Part II, that I would stop dropping my jaw to the ground each time the next amazing "coincidence" occurs, but each instance never ceases to blow my mind, or make me shout "no way." I also cannot believe when I look back at patterns and see that if this one little minor thing did not occur, then there is no way "all the stars" would have aligned and this would all have been possible. So before I get into the details about the progress over the year, let me first tell you about my return visit to London one year later…

RETURN VISIT TO LONDON

Let me start by saying that because I sold my business and since all of these spiritual signs started occurring for me, I have spent a lot of time travelling to and educating myself about sacred sites. I also took the time over the year to do all the training and started a travel agency, so that I would not only be able to benefit my own travel, but take others to these amazing places and educate them after I have my initial reconnaissance tours myself. All that being said, I obviously know how to get pretty decent rates for hotel rooms for myself, especially as an agent. However on my return trip to London, I booked very late, so unfortunately the best rates were not that good in central London and many places were not even offering an "agent rate." I took my lumps and reserved a room for only a couple nights in the well-situated central location of Trafalger Square. I chose the square because I immediately remembered that it is where the four huge lion statues are located, how appropriate, right?

> Please remember that when I tell you facts about my journey, as always, it will seem like I am way off subject, but I just have to present the facts in the order they actually occurred and let synchronicities to the lion unfold for themselves at the end.

Well the hotel common areas were pretty modern and clean, but the rooms were hideous quality for the cost, old and dirty carpets, strange smells, etc. I checked in at night and I am travelling alone, so immediately I go to close the curtains. The ceiling is high and the track on the curtain had been hung back up by maintenance even though the track was all bent up. So I gave the curtain a little tug to close, and the entire curtain and the rod came down crashing on top of my head. One thing I have learned this year is that when I have setbacks along the way I have to immediately keep my mind focused on the fact that there is a reason for everything that occurs in life and how my thoughts reacting to these setbacks will determine whether the outcome is positive or negative. It is a little difficult when it becomes painful, and we will not repeat in public my immediate reaction when it first hit me. However, I have come a long way from a year ago and I got my composure in a few seconds and remembered my attitude is critical. So I thought to myself "there is reason for this, and something good is going to come from it." I walk to the front desk and politely express my feelings saying "I am trying to stay calm and not get angry but I am in some pain from this thing hitting me on the head, and it was irresponsible to hang it back up when it was obvious the track was no longer adequate to hold the curtain." Then I state "it is all fine, but I will not sleep in a room without a curtain, so you have to move me." They reception desk tells me they are sold out of rooms for the night. I do not give up faith that something good is supposed to happen and I say softly "well find a manager and see if you can still move me before everyone else checks-in because I do not want a maintenance crew in the room while I am going to bed and I do not want to wake up with blinding sun in my eyes." In the back of my mind, I am thinking they are probably only sold out of my standard class room and my rate, but have other rooms available that were out of my price range. She tells me to wait in the lounge. Then a manager comes over to offer to move me to another room and help me with my luggage. In my mind, I am thinking "thank you angels", the hotel must be taking me to one of those special upgrade rooms that they could not sell for the night.

Well the second room, if you can believe it was downgrade. It had the same dirty carpets even on a different floor of the hotel, smaller bed, smaller everything, etc. Hey I think to myself "it is all I need, I am here on a mission to check on the lion, this is not about me." I settle in. I discover after talking with the zoo and trying to make plans for meetings with other potential supporters that I probably will in fact be staying in London longer. So the next day I decide I am going to move hotels, things had gotten even a little worse. Call me a snob or whatever, but I was missing my clean home and feeling like bug bed central was what I had slept on. I go to the business center and decide to surf and check rates myself using my travel agent access. There was only one card that I happened to have with me overseas to give me my access number for another chain. But I knew that their hotel in London was the top of the line (a place I knew was known for celebrities and high tea etc.), so I was not holding my breath for that. I would expect their rates to be three times what I was paying. But it was the only card number I had with me, so curiosity, intuition, whatever I checked it out. Seriously, the room offered to me that particular night was $100 Euro cheaper per night than were I was staying. Get out! Of course, I would take a hit in the head by curtain rod any day to stay in that hotel, just bring it. Thank you universe, for acknowledging that I knew there was something better coming (power of positive thinking cannot go wrong). Moving on up (imagine an American football dance in your head, cause I was doing it).

I am not a stranger to the hotel, because I had been there before on a previous visit and had the opportunity to enjoy high tea with a friend, so I knew what I was looking forward to, and I personally consider it one of the best hotels in London. So my first night in my luxury accommodations I head down to the lobby to check everything out. I run into a gentleman dressed in a tuxedo and he makes a comment that I have a nice jumper. Americans do not typically know what a "jumper" is and I had just learnt that meaning within the last 24 hours (there are no coincidences). Otherwise, I probably would have made a strange face and said "huh." Instead I thanked him and said oh you like my sweater. He said "yes", are you Norwegian. I said "no", but you are dead on, it is a Norwegian sweater. I said "I am American."

He asked what I was doing in London. Now you need to know that I have just spent two weeks travelling to sacred sites all over Ireland, and therefore I could have told him anything. But I said "I had started a campaign to save animals in captivity and the London zoo is my first project." He said "you are kidding me." When I assured him it was true, he next thanked me for doing that. Then he asked if by any chance I had a dress in my suitcase and would I like to attend a black tie event occurring in my hotel that night for animal rights! He said it would be inspiring for others to see an American here doing something for their zoo and that he would like to introduce me to others that may be able to help my cause. I am thinking "pinch me, is this really happening." He said I could come as his guest, and I ran upstairs to raid through my luggage. I had one sort of dressy outfit, but it clearly would give the statement that this lady has no idea how to dress for a black tie affair. I know no one and this is a black tie event at one of the most glamorous hotels in London, and I am well aware that as a general rule the British have a lot more concern about dress code and etiquette. However, I have that little angel "sitting on my shoulder" that reminds me that my name Tracy means "courage", great. I made the only "very American" move I felt feasible, I threw on my dress blue jeans, a sequenced nice top, a pair of heels, put my hair up in twist and went downstairs to crash the event. I was feeling bold. I marched up to the door of the event and completely chickened out, especially after I saw a couple of the sequence gowns passing me. I was standing there outside the event doors with the butlers asking if they might be able to help me locate someone and get them a message. I was thinking I would just wait in the lobby bar until everyone was done and then try to catch them. Then my new friend came out the door like magic and caught me there being indecisive, and said "I was wondering what took you so long." I apologized for my appearance, and the next thing I knew I was getting a tour of the auction items and introduced to amazing philanthropists and other not-for-profit organizations that help animals. They even had vegan food for me! Magic, pure magical evening, all because a curtain rod hit me in the head.

Best of all, I had held one of my meetings with the zoo that morning, and so I had all the flyers and marketing materials with me to help "my lions" and information about upcoming gala events to support my campaign.

So if you remember, in Part II of this book I spoke highly of my now good friend Mr. Sangha and his connection to a wonderful man, Lord Paul. I will tell you about how my connection to his family started to grow, in a minute, but first I must expose my ignorance and state that I really had no idea up until now what a Lord actually was.

Well my new friends at the black tie event taught me about how the government functions for England. I realize they have a Parliament and House of Lords, comprised of Members of Parliament and Lords. I relate them to our Senators and Congressman, even though the structure and powers are very different. So I now realized that Lord Paul was an appointed representative of the House of Lords and that my new friend that had taken me under his wing as a guest was actually a Member of Parliament. I just happened to be sitting with the Member of Parliament that was recently instrumental in getting a law passed to stop the abuse of animals in circuses. In addition, Lord Paul is one of the greatest supporters of the London zoo through my understanding from Mr. Sangha speaking so highly of him. I have both forms of government brought to me by the universe to hear the need. It was unbelievable, but yet here I was living it. Who could still call these coincidences?

I also want to apologize, because I could never write enough to tell you about "all" of the synchronicities that are happening along this "illuminated" path for me, otherwise I would stop living them just to keep up with the writing.

So on this return to London, one of the meetings that I had scheduled was to take Mr. Sangha to meet with the development and philanthropic directors at the zoo. It amazingly opened another door. Mr. Sangha is related to the Sikh community and from India. He has been a supporter of a not-for-profit organization helping to build schools for education. He was not as familiar with animal needs, but extremely kind hearted and willing to help and be instrumental in introductions to the right people however possible. During the tour of the London zoo, to show him the conditions of the lion habitat, the zoo made a connection to him explaining that there only about 400 remaining Asiatic lions in the wild all in one small geographic area in India. As you will read below, the zoo has been focused on conservation efforts to maintain the wild habitat in India for these lions and help train veterinarians in India to help these magnificent creatures. But the zoo does not receive funding in return yet from the Indian government, so I am hopeful that Mr. Sangha will be able to help with some connections, and if is it meant to be, it will happen. I knew they were Asiatic, but I had no idea until this trip where the remaining wild habitat was located. What are the chances?

Now I want to share something profoundly personal for me, and very moving in my heart. As I walked through the zoo with Mr. Sangha, he knew what he was looking for, even though he did not say a word, he immediately approached a statue and asked if we would take his photo with the statue. This was the statue of Lord Paul's daughter who had passed away when she was only five years old. I looked at the statue and I could not believe my eyes. The young girl who loved animals was holding her hand up in the air and there was a bird in her hand. I do not know where to begin about how significant this is for me, but I am going to show you through pictures.

I have to go back several years, when I was running my design firm and driving myself crazy from the stress and rigorous demands. I had gone through a divorce and bad business partnership. So one weekend I read about a yoga retreat and just decided to take off for Ocala National Forest and participate. I was mostly worried about whether I was in good enough shape to keep up with other partcipants, my body had really begun to atrophy on the left side from stress. I did not really give it a second thought that it was called a "Goddess" Yoga Retreat. I always feel like the world comes up with "cutsie" adjectives for everything, like the names of colors. However, it just so happened that this retreat was organized by a group of, I guess you would say "intuitives", from Jamaica. I am extremely open-minded to all of that now. But we are going back when I was the successful President of a company, living in a black and white world only focused on survival and making money with integrity. Sadly, spiritual issues were never researched or really even discussed around me. Looking back and thinking about it, I was miserable, empty and a huge success.

So this yoga retreat offers some yoga, some group meditation sessions and roughing it and sleeping on floors. No big deal, right? That is what I expected. Then you add in that it has mandatory body painting, group all girl dancing, tarot cards and last but not least painting on canvases. Now I am out of my element completely. What, what? I am here in the middle of the woods. I am not a party pooper, and it is too far to drive back home for the night comfortably, so just join them is my attitude. I have to say the body painting, dancing and giggling is not to be missed – treasured memories. Lastly, comes this required painting. The Jamaican ladies give us these detailed instructions to channel our "inner goddess" and paint whatever comes to mind. What? I had no idea what "channel" meant. But I said the prayer words they recommended with the group and just started painting. I realized I was sort of painting a goddess, as you can see in the picture below. I painted a yellow color all around her body. I had never heard of an aura or chakra in my whole life. But now I know well that what I painted looks like an aura and yellow represents our emotional solar plexus chakra. She had a crown like a princess, but no face. She was standing beside what I would now call the "tree of life", since on this trip I discovered the Crowe family crest (my namesake) is the tree of life. That was interesting. **Lastly, and most important she is holding that bird in her hand like the statue in the zoo.** So we get done painting, and these Jamaican ladies say that we are going to walk up and lay both of our hands on our paintings, ask our inner goddess to channel us and turn around and say or act out the first thing that comes to mind. One of them went first, and her picture sort of had serpentine lines going up and down a female figure. So the Jamaican lady held her hands on her painting and then turned around and started moving herself like a snake and making a hissing sound, but then she said something profound that I have completely forgotten. I was too nervous. "Oh no", I am thinking with my 'monkey mind' running a million miles an hour. Of course, I get called on next. So I go up to my painting, touch it with both hands like they said, ask my inner Goddess to channel me (when I have no freaking clue what the definition of

53

channeling is) and wait. I had a wave of emotion rush throughout my body. Then I slowly turn around. I am literally sobbing, crying so hard I can barely see and just looking at all of these women in the group on the floor saying over and over "it's OK, it's going to be OK, it's all OK." I was hysterical and embarrassed to no end when I sat back down and then I hear whispers "oh, she's a plant (meaning some of the other ladies in the group think that I was "paid" by the Jamaican ladies as an actress). Really, how much could yoga instructors pay the President of a company with no acting background for that kind of thing? I left really bewildered about what had just happened, but I have to share two quick ironies – I was later to get a project through my company redoing the civil engineering for a port design in Jamaica and this year I took acting classes for the first time ever and I am already in a movie that is filming in Florida in my backyard. I did not even know we produced movies in Florida… It is a brand new independent film maker. All I know is there are no coincidences in life.

Now, back at the Zoo that day in London, I walked up to the statue of the little girl with the bird and read what is said on the plaque about Ambika Paul, Lord Swraj Paul's daughter. My heart stopped beating and I felt like all of the oxygen was gone from the planet. I knew she passed on at five years old from leukemia, but I thought it was just in recent years. She died one year before I was born. I had goosebumps, chills and basically kinesis energy flowing all over my body. I know there is no mistake that this sweet little energy has some influence over me to this day and she has used it to bring me here to her blessed zoo. God bless her and God bless this lion that took on the name of the Lightbearer to hopefully make a difference for animals in captivity for many years to come. I will be here to help them carry the torch all I can. I cannot help but shed a tear now as I read her dedication plaque on the statue at the zoo which states "Ambika was an angel who changed our lives."

I am a changed person from all of this. The business suits are in the back of the closet now. Did I mention that I got a push to go and get my license to become a Reverend. Why not? There is nothing that makes my heart sing more than thinking I spoke to someone and know they feel closer to the love of their creator and they are grateful to me for simply being and sharing. It has nothing to do with Sunday, or religion or starting a congregation. The connection is direct. It is simply finding our creator in the everyday signs of life and migrating through our own hearts to find our calling and then sharing the news of those blessings with those ready to hear it.

A NEW CHARITY FOR ANIMALS IN CAPTIVITY

So what else positive has occurred since my first encounter with Lucifer the Lion? Well I took the campaign a bit further, and became determined to start a charity for animals in captivity. So my lion did actually get that number and name for a specific purpose, Lucifer will be a Lightbearer and his existence will help other animals in captivity. I am hoping to do a documentary as well as to help more animals based upon this lightbearer's story, before we all become myth and folklore…maybe that is why our creator placed signs in front of me to encourage acting classes.

I have Big plans for the charity, besides focusing on getting better habitats for animals. I want to help fund "no kill" facilities (in other words facilities that take in strays, abandoned and abused animals but will not put them to sleep). I want to help people in communities that fall on hard times and cannot feed their animals (but only providing healthy animal food, not money directly). I also want to help facilities that have rescued animals from sports and from entertainment venues. I do not see any one animal as more valuable than another type. They all have specific needs.

Another project that came to mind with the new charity is standards for development of animal habitats that are appropriate for their species. I remembered from all my years of running my design firm and working as an expert for governments that there are standards now that we develop for schools such as minimum acreage per school site, and standards that we develop for parks such as minimum acreage per type of park that we require governments in the USA to adhere to. However, most countries have either very minimal standards for habitats or none. The standards have been more focused on human safety than animal quality of life. I want the charity to work with organizations and governments to develop absolute minimum standards for the quality of life of wild animals that are held in captivity.

The charity that I established with a group of volunteers is called CaptivityAngels, Inc. It is pretty exhilarating. My friend from Parliament introduced me to an organization called BornFree to get assistance with running an organization and I will tell you more about them and that amazing encounter in a section below.

As you saw on the front cover, **all of the proceeds** from the sale of this book and I mean all that come to me as author will go to animals in captivity, so please smile at yourself in the mirror you did a really good thing buying this book. I am praying that this book will sell for years to help animals around the world, but I will continue to start other projects and ventures to add to the capital for the charity.

INTRODUCTION TO ZSL AND THE LONDON ZOO

Next, let me take this opportunity to introduce you to the Zoological Society of London (ZSL). It is charity itself that was established in 1826. This charity is focused on promoting the worldwide conservation of animals and their habitats. They work in over 50 countries. A lot of their conservation efforts are focused on animals nearing extinction, learning and teaching about them, but more importantly trying to bring an awareness to destruction of their habitats and keep those left in the wild safe. There is much to read about their research and conservation at www.zsl.org under the conservation tab.

However, ZSL also operates the London Zoo and Whipsnade Zoo. As I mentioned in Part I, they receive very little statutory funding from the government and I am sure it is harder on the government with the recent recession. ZSL gets the majority of its funds for habitat rebuilding and conservation projects through the generosity of supporters and visitors to the zoo, **in other words from us**. Unfortunately, the zoo is not a free entry fee, but at least it is one of the tourist locations that are included in the London Pass.

I was very torn regarding some issues, as ZSL is every year when they have to look at their own budget. When you are faced with the decision, do I support research in an underprivileged area of the world to stop an entire community of animals from going extinct OR do I put money into rebuilding the antiquated habitats for the animals in our own facilities, it is a tough decision every year. When I first came upon the scene during the Olympics, all of their focus was on the tiger habitat reconstruction, so there was not even a design in place for the lion enclosure. Part of the issue is that the enclosure was already inadequate size for a pride of lions and now they had just had **cubs**.

One year later the zoo has completed the new state of art Tiger exhibit space and had developed a beautiful new design to greatly expand the lion habitat area, and raise people off the ground level to go on bridges above the exhibit area and give that space back to the lions.

Here is the bottom line and the issue I became faced with after campaigning and offering to help finance the construction of a new lion enclosure. The zoo bred those cubs, when they did not have adequate habitat for their parents. Once bred in captivity, the cubs do not know how to hunt and are too acclimated to humans to be released back into the wild. Therefore, the Zoo's policy to allow breeding is perpetuating the life of the king of the beasts behind bars in an inadequate facility. If my charity helps them build a larger habitat, I fear that they may simply buy animals or keep breeding to put more in captivity for commercial use. One could say that these lions that people pay to see are raising money to save others in the wild. However, the same people paying to go to the zoo "are us", and we could instead be paying to help animals in the wild and those sanctuaries that are truly rescuing animals without increasing the number in captivity.

I have been waking up at night crying with spirit working through my dreams, and making me realize how wrong it is to contribute to the continued breeding at this zoo even though I feel personally and deeply attached to this lion family in London. I have learnt a lot in the past year, I realize that the $5.7 million Euro that ZSL is asking for to re-build the habitat is grossly exuberant. Rescue sanctuaries in the US that want to build large turnouts for big cats have asked me for as little as $12,173, but they do a lot with volunteers. The rescue facilities are not high end, typically grass and trees, but the lions mostly need room to run. Regardless, the dilemma is apparent, that $5.7 million Euro is not logical for even a state of the art facility. I am not saying that ZSL would not use the extra funds for very good causes. I just know that the $3 million Euro already raised is enough for an outstanding lion habitat.

My plan is to stay true to my word and on May 21, 2014 at the Zoo's Gala offer the original $25,000 to ZSL for the lion habitat, if they will agree to sign a document that they will stop breeding the lions in captivity and will not buy any animals from commercial breeders and put them in captivity. You will have to go to our website www.captivityangels.org to keep up with our social media and see what happens. If ZSL refuses to stop breeding, my charity will donate the $25,000 to the animal rescue charities that I am already trying to raise money to assist.

There are many abused and abandoned animals euthanized every day, because there is no facility to rescue them. Most Zoo's are not rescuing these abused animals, they are purchasing animals or dragging them out of the wild into cages. "We", you and I, are responsible for this because we create the market demand.

BORNFREE

BornFree is an international organization focused on ending the suffering of wild animals and actively pursues efforts to encourage compassionate conservation globally. They use powerful tools including legislation, public education, litigation and grassroots networking. For example, related to the cause of helping highly endangered lion species, here are just a few examples:

- Building Bomas to help the Kenyan Wildlife Service build safety enclosures to separate people and their livestock from lion habitat conflict areas. This necessary separation will greatly reduce hunts to kill lions.
- Rescuing lions in Ethiopia from illegal ownership or from trade, many in deplorable conditions. If they can be released back in the wild, that will happen. There are 20 lions they are trying to raise funds to rescue right now from the Addis Abada zoo that are in tiny cages with bars.
- An education program about the conservation of the species through Ethopian schools, nature clubs and universities.
- Proposing legislation against the raising, slaughter, the sales of lion meat for human consumption that I previously mentioned.
- There are animals currently in desperate need of transport to Wildlife preserves and sanctuaries. Bornfree offers animals some of their first opportunities to stretch their legs in the wild as their bodies were designed by God to do.

I was introduced to some of the amazing individuals that are running this organization in my hotel in London at the black tie fund raising event that I mentioned I was invited to above. This organization does not support zoos, circuses or any type of urban enclosures for wild animals because of the frequent abuse it has led to in many situations and the inadequacies. So now the universe had opened a door for me and offered me a big brother organization to show me all the ropes in growing my organization to the professional caliber that it will need to withstand to help around the world.

This includes providing access to their amazing library of resources. Remember that I stated I wanted to develop standards for habitat design? Well, BornFree has worked extensively to get the European Commission to agree to a request to develop a 'best practice' zoo guide to assist zoo operators to meet the legal requirements for habitats. I love these people. Their website has an amazing display of country reports and investigations of the adequacy or inadequacy of current animal enclosures in zoos, and the website is growing with new reports. There is an opportunity for the public to report inadequacies and/or abuse of animals directly to them for help.

So let me tell you the last "major" synchronicity about the lion before this book is pried from my hands to go to publish. I met the BornFree organization **in London**. They discovered I was from the USA and said let us invite you to meet with our BornFreeUSA representative in the States. He is located in Washington DC. I said "you are kidding, that is my hometown, and I will be passing through there on my way back home to Florida to visit with my family." So I called their representative and he would be more than happy to get together and discuss my charity. Then, I realized that I would only be in DC Friday night to Monday morning and I need to spend time with my mother during the weekend which is an hour and half away from DC and I usually stay there over night. So the odds were stacking up against this meeting, but I really wanted to make this connection now. I was praying that he worked weekends, etc. Then the next small miracle took place. His home on the weekends is 10 minutes from my Mother's location. So we attended an Apple Butter Festival together with both of our families and set down and had a professional meeting over coffee while they walked around. It was perfect.

There is one last major focus area that I want to discuss about this amazing organization that the universe put right in my path. Inadequate facilities for animals are one issue, but abuse or misuse of any animal is a completely different issue. If you ever see any form of abuse or misuse of animals there are many resources for you to contact to MAKE A DIFFERENCE yourself. Once you see it, it becomes your responsibility too. That is why you were present to see it; there are no coincidences in life. I am not saying take police action or fight fire with fire. I am not even saying start a campaign or charity like did, unless it is your calling. Please I implore you though, do not ignore animal abuse. They are much more helpless than we are. We are their voice. It is our responsibility. Take time to report it to an organization like BornFree, and I will show you how to do that in the next section.

HOW TO HELP RESCUE ANIMALS AND CONSERVE HABITAT IMMEDIATELY

Animals are rescued every day by amazing people that truly care for their wellbeing. But the cost for care for the lifespan of these animals can be enormous. Our charity is currently working with rescuers around the world to save elephants, monkeys, dogs, tigers, lions, bears, horses, owls, parrots, cats, etc.

If you would like to donate to my new CaptivityAngels charity, please go to www.captivityangels.org. Your proceeds will go to sanctuaries that truly love animals, do not allow breeding in tiny inadequate facilities and do not buy animals commercially for entertainment. You will be able to track the progress of our projects and your donations on the website and our social media sites. What will be especially unique about this charity? We are going to use the latest technology and donors will be provided with a code/password whether they donate $100 or $1,000,000. They will be able to go onto our website and enter their code/password and it will show them exactly which animals in which facilities received their generous donation. In addition, donors will feel excellent about their gift because they will be able to rest assured that the funding from our charity goes directly to contractors for construction of new facilities, or to purchase food or veterinarian supplies and not to the owners of the facilities for administrative costs.

What will be especially unique about this charity? We are going to use the latest technology and donors will be provided with a code whether they donate $100 or $1,000,000. They will be able to go onto our website and enter their code and it will show them exactly which animals in which facilities received their generous donation. In addition, donors will feel excellent about their gift because they will be able to rest assured that the funding from our charity goes directly to contractors for construction of new facilities, or to purchase food or veterinarian supplies and **not to the owners of the facilities for administrative costs.**

Also, the habitat for many animals in the wild has tremendously reduced. For instance, there are estimated to be less than 400 rare Asiatic lions left in the wild. They are all located in one isolated geographic area of western India, known as the Gir Forest Protected Area. The primary cause of death for the lions, at over 40%, is linked to conflicts with humans, and the human-wildlife interaction is escalating. It is the largest challenge to overcome for lion conservation. If you would like to find out more or donate to conservation efforts and support the BornFree organization. Please go to www.BornFree.com for more information and how to help. Any form of witnessed animal abuse or misuse should also be reported to this organization and/or your local police if it is a domestic animal.

CONCLUSION

I hope that this will demonstrate that an individual can make a huge difference. I just followed the signs and my intuition and had the courage to tell people about a good cause. I think I have demonstrated that if you keep faith and your thoughts positive, it is absolutely true that you get support from the universe and the doors begin to open for you. But also how we need each other to accomplish worthy projects and how the universe brings the right people together to get it all done.

I mentioned that this is not actually my first book, but because of the need I had to go ahead and push this one through first. Be on the lookout for *Awakening of an Indigo* soon.

EPILOGUE

I have been granted the gift of learning so much through my astrology training and watching this world transform from the Age of Pisces to the Age of Aquarius. So many mysteries that have been sung about for so many years, such as the "dawning of the Age of Aquarius" sang in the 1960's, are starting to reveal themselves. They always say the universe puts spiritual messages right out in the open, but we never ask what it means.

I truly believe with all my heart that I am witnessing many of us going through an awakening to a new age of humanitarian focus. I can see it in the past decade of the "green movement", the changes in all of the grocery stores and profound new awareness of mother earth. So many people everywhere are starting to focus on breathing, chakra's, meditation and learning compassion for each other. More importantly, we know intuitively it is the right path to follow.

It is time for us to include the animal kingdom in this new reality. Nature is complex and we are learning that every living thing has a soul and connection to mother earth. We have to follow our inner truth to prevent more atrocities and violence toward the animal kingdom. We must stop getting distracted by the outer world of politics, social rules and religion that were created by us through an illusion of fear. It is time to stand in our power and know the truth that we are inherently beings of Peace and Love.

Author Reverend Tracy Crowe with Dr. Arun Gandhi the grandson of Mahatma Gandhi in humble gratitude and support of his nonviolence campaign for animal rights at Christ Church Unity in Orlando.

ABOUT THE AUTHOR

Reverend Tracy L. Crowe is a spiritual pilgrim that has a deep compassion for animals. She is a writer, an actress, a travel agent, an astrologer and messenger of affirmations. Rev. Crowe was formerly the successful owner of a private design consulting firm, Land Design Innovations, Inc., which was recognized as one of the largest woman-owned businesses in Central Florida in 2011. She now manages several companies under the umbrella of TLC Consulting Services, LLC; including her new most prized company, CaptivityAngels to help animals in inadequate facilities and poor conditions.

Printed in the United States
By Bookmasters